RECOVER
REBUILD
Thrive

Praise for

Recover, Rebuild, Thrive

'I am impressed by Christiana's insight, her extensive knowledge of psychological strategies and her ability to empathise with people affected by difficult change. Her self-help book *Recover, Rebuild, Thrive* is not only inspirational but also offers practical guidance to a wide range of readers'. – *Beatriz Copello, PhD, Psychologist, Author and Playwright*

'Christiana's skill lies with her ability to break down complex issues into their key components. She understands that people who are going through difficult situations need information, clarity and practical advice. *Recover, Rebuild, Thrive* has a real-world approach that I find extremely engaging'. – *Susie Hamilton. Small business owner, single parent*

'Full of strengthening words of wisdom and great comfort when needed'. – *Catherine Smith, Writer and Poet*

'Christiana has the capacity to bring real insight into your circumstances and has the compassion to lead you through your inner journey at your own pace'. – *Karen La Fou, Business Banker*

'*Recover, Rebuild, Thrive* is realistic, practical and positive. It is not only a valuable addition to your personal collection, as a reference book, but would be a caring and loving gift to give to anyone you know who is suffering from psychological stress'. – *Mary Ann Napper. Author of* Born to Fly

'I love how the real stories illustrate strategies and how they help to support recovery. The content is well organised and presents a very comprehensive range of exercises and techniques in a way that is informative and reader friendly. I will certainly recommend the book to appropriate clients'. – *Debbie Cameron, Psychologist*

'Each chapter comes alive for me because of the case studies that really help me see the relevance of each chapter. *Recover, Rebuild, Thrive* is full of common sense and I also love all the tips and hints. I thoroughly recommend this book. It doesn't matter whether you are going through a change or not because this book will absolutely touch different parts of your life'. – *Sue Heins, Local Government Representative and Owner of Business Women's Networking Group*

RECOVER REBUILD
Thrive

A practical guide for moving on
from difficult life changes

CHRISTIANA STAR

This edition published in 2018 by WiseStar*Publishing

Cover design by Farrah Careem

Ebook ISBN: 9781925786217

Print on demand ISBN: 9781925786224

Contents

Introduction

This book is about change. About external changes that arrive in our lives uninvited and the internal changes necessary to adapt and move on. As a psychologist in private practice this is something with which I have much experience. I also consulted in corporate settings when difficult situations arose: redundancies, accidents, death or suicide of a work colleague, armed hold-ups, abuse and many other critical incidents.

The number of sessions allocated to help the individuals through their experiences was always very limited. They needed something to help them afterwards. As a former teacher I had the skills to develop individually tailored programs clients could use to help themselves. By necessity and inclination I became a very practical psychologist.

My own life journey also had its share of challenges. Two car accidents - none of them my fault - cancer and other illnesses, PTSD, relocating from Germany to Australia and change of profession showed me on a very personal level what it takes to recover and rebuild yourself, and ultimately thrive after difficult changes and adversity.

Every person's path to renewed health and wholeness is different depending on the specifics of the experience, its nature, intensity and duration, the degree of personal resilience and the support afterwards.

However, irrespective of individual differences, picking up the pieces, starting from scratch and re-inventing yourself and your life is like a puzzle of many different fragments coming together. Troubling symptoms need to be addressed, an authentic sense of self restored, intense emotions managed, dysfunctional thinking overcome, relationships negotiated and new life skills activated. But it is much more than that.

While adversity usually includes some form of loss, it also contains the seeds for positive transformation. Both aspects need our attention but the one chosen as the main guiding light determines the future.

One response is to give up in resignation and see the experience as something devastating, never to be recovered from and putting an end to all happiness and a satisfying life. The other choice is more difficult. It requires the willingness and persistence to not only adapt to changed circumstances but more importantly to take full responsibility for our responses and inner life.

This book shows readers how to help themselves for rejuvenation and transformation. Pathways to successful change are illustrated by stories of real-life cases. Names and identifying details of the people involved, as well as their circumstances, have been modified to guarantee anonymity. I encountered the individuals as clients in my private practice or at the many critical incidents I attended. Each 'story' was chosen to represent one particular aspect of self-change. Life circumstances and other people involved are included for clarity where needed but the stories are told with particular focus on my clients. We meet most of them in two places in the book: in the beginning to demonstrate strategies for recovery and rebuilding, and later on in updates showing their way towards thriving.

The book is organised into two parts.

Part 1, Recover and Rebuild is about making a fresh start. The individual chapters deal with:

- The foundational skills needed for navigating change successfully (1).
- Different techniques from many multi-disciplinary fields for calming an overwhelmed nervous system and relieving the physical symptoms of stress (2).
- Discussion and strategies for dealing with loss and grief (3).
- Stress-induced depression, anger and anxiety (4,5,6).
- Changing automatic thoughts and dysfunctional beliefs (7).
- Improving the relationship you have with yourself and standing your ground when challenged (8, 9).
- How to take the initiative and create your own change within the changes imposed on you by external events (10).

Part 2, Thrive, is about completing the transformative journey:

- Guidance for healing painful memories and practising forgiveness (11).
- Building emotional stability (12).
- Living with authenticity and personal power (13, 14).
- Advanced skills for mastering future changes (15).

- Creating new meaning and purpose (16).
- The closing thoughts - Make sure your psychological toolkit is up-to-date - provide a summary of the skills and perspectives needed for successful transformation.

A word of warning. Be mindful of the stage you are at. If your experience is still very raw and your distress substantial, it is probably too early to embark on substantial inner work. Consult chapter 2 (Calm The Body) and practise the self-soothing exercises and perhaps also use the technique for riding out emotional storms (chapter 12). Leave the structured and reflective work until you feel more settled.

This book presents a comprehensive roadmap for self-change. While its primary focus is the aftermath of difficult life changes, it can also be useful reading for anyone who feels the need for personal transformation and is unsure how to go about it. Read it as a whole or use as a reference when only certain chapters are important or relevant to your own situation.

The message of the book is one of hope and assurance that adversity does not need to destroy you and irrevocably reduce your chances at a satisfying and productive life.

Going beyond loss and damage, you can foster positive new developments, discover unexpected openings, review your attitudes, expand your perspectives and reset priorities. The scars from your experience may remain but your internal and outer lives do not need to be defined by them. Instead you can use your experience as a catalyst for extraordinary transformation and grow into a person with great inner strength, emotional freedom and self-determination.

Part 1

Recover And Rebuild

Chapter 1

Build Strong Foundations

Change rarely follows a straightforward path. Often it is like an obstacle course proceeding in three main phases. The first one is full of endings: things that had been part of your life may no longer be available or possible. Second is a middle zone where you are moving forward into a new direction, but are also still bound by the past. This makes it an often uncomfortable and turbulent space to be in, particularly if you have not chosen the change or it is irreversible. The third phase is characterised by real new beginnings.

You may be going back and forth between the phases, with stops and starts, perhaps three steps forward and two back, disappointments and achievements, upheavals and calmness.

If significant and painful life changes have rattled your sense of self, you may be struggling to know who you are in the new conditions. Facing serious issues and having to adapt to new limitations often means that parts of the 'old you' have to be modified and a 'new you' developed.

Lucy's story

Lucy had a great life. She loved her work, her partner, her large network of friends and close-knit family. But recently Lucy was not quite herself. Unusually tired and uncomfortable with various aches and pains, she often felt like resting rather than going out as she was used to doing. And the pains - she must have inadvertently hurt herself at the gym, it had happened before. Whatever it was, right now it seemed comforting and sensible to rest when she could. She wanted to get back on track as quickly as possible.

But things did not improve. Lucy could not shake the fatigue despite going to bed earlier and sleeping longer. Work had become very tiring and her absences increased. She just did not seem to have much energy and the aches lingered. Just focusing and getting things done was a major effort. This was not normal. After consulting with her doctor, and many tests and meetings with specialists, the eventual diagnosis was severe. A rare form of autoimmune disorder with few treatment options, uncertain progress and recovery not guaranteed.

Lucy was shattered; her life had just fallen apart. She had always been an energetic person, vivacious and fun loving. Who was she now - an invalid for the rest of her life? Everything in her rebelled; she was furious and cursed her fate. Why did this happen to her? She had always looked after herself; she did not deserve such a blow. The life she had envisaged and planned for was in shambles. What about her travel plans? Would she be able to continue work? Would her friends stand by her now she couldn't join in with them as before? The future looked uncertain and very frightening.

Accept reality

Most of us believe that life should be a certain way and unfold in the way we imagine. We expect a certain outcome if we work hard, are good people, do everything right. But when we are side-swiped by unexpected occurrences such expectations are shattered. To accept the new circumstances without rebelling seems tantamount to surrender to unseen and threatening forces. So we fight against the events in our lives, telling ourselves that we cannot manage the new order of things.

To roll with life's punches we need to accept the reality of the situation rather than wishing it were different. That does not mean giving up but means taking proactive measures for moving forward.

Lucy struggled with the new circumstances particularly as her automatic thoughts seemed so true: *all is lost, my life is finished, not even the doctors know how to deal with this, I'll never get over this.* Trying to find an explanation for why it happened she even got stuck in 'analysis paralysis'. But dwelling on the 'why' was not going to help her, as sometimes there is no obvious reason why difficult things happen. Lucy's real challenge was finding the 'how': how to live with her disease, how not to loose herself in it, how to move forward from here.

Any difficult life change brings with it new challenges. It's natural to focus on the difficulties or dwell on the factors that contributed to the event but convincing as they may be, such thoughts are often unrealistic, over-dramatic, fear-based or simply wrong. They also have a negative impact on emotions, increasing a sense of helplessness, loss of hope, despair and loneliness.

Choose your perspective

Fortunately, after a period of distress and feeling overwhelmed, Lucy was able to tap into a source of strength within herself. Reminded by family and friends of previous challenges she had overcome, she realised that she was not as powerless as it seemed and the outcome of her current predicament was not set in stone.

Lucy began by taking a broader, more detached view of the situation. As if looking down from a helicopter, she viewed her predicament from a wider perspective:

- *Does the experience determine my whole future and condemn me to lifelong misery?*

- *Is the event a total catastrophe or a stumbling block I can deal with?*

- *Is it a reason to cower, shrivel and stagnate or a starting point to rustle up all my resources, pick up the pieces and find a way forward?*

- *Who am I: a victim or a resilient person who despite the odds can overcome this challenge?*

- *I am wounded but not completely broken.*

- *There is a part of me that remains whole even in the new circumstance.*

- *I can find a way to improve and move on from this.*

- *I can rebuild my life and redefine who I am.*

- *Other people have experienced something similar and gone on to greater strength and a rewarding life.*

- *I will find people who support my healing.*

- *Even though life is terribly difficult at the moment, there can be lighter moments as well.*

- *I will use my current situation as a starting point for a new beginning.*

Focus on solutions

In her distress, Lucy had let herself go, lost interest in her appearance and drifted through the days as a helpless invalid. But now, with renewed resolve not to lose her old spark, she began to focus on lifting her spirits and restoring some sense of normalcy.

A place to rest was set up in her lounge room so she was no longer confined and isolated in her bedroom for long periods. Lucy had always enjoyed photography and began taking her camera with her when she went out. It was actually quite enjoyable to download the images later and post them on social media. It kept her in the loop and maintained the conversation with her friends. She also began taking short walks when feeling better and stopped in a nearby coffeeshop when she needed a break or just to talk to people. Back home, she spent much time researching her illness and potential options for healing.

Focusing on solutions does not necessarily mean finding big answers to big problems. When things are complicated and full of handicaps, look for what is do-able at any given time, one step at a time. Even if there seems to be an impenetrable brick wall in front of you, look for openings or ways around it. No matter how insignificant an action may be, if the conditions are right it can have a big impact.

Work with everything you can control. Consider your particular problems and ask yourself: *can I change anything about it right now?* If the answer is *no,* accept it as a fact for now and trust that there will be an opening in the future. If the answer is *yes* or *maybe,* consider your options. They might include making physical changes or adjustments, repairing a damaged relationship, learning self-calming techniques, enlisting help, or any other positive steps that could improve your situation.

Self-responsibility - burden or power?

When life is challenging, it is common to speak as if events or other people have the power to determine your emotions: *he makes me sad, people make me so angry, being like this makes me want to give up altogether.* However, nobody can 'make' you feel, think or act in certain ways unless you allow it. Events may be beyond your control, but how you respond is your choice:

- what you do with your feelings and emotions - lose yourself in them or take action to rein them in?

- what thoughts you give importance to - negative or realistic and proactive?

- where you put your attention - on what is lost or what you can build on?

- your beliefs - are they dragging you down or lifting you up?

- the companions you choose and how you interact with them

- your well-being, happiness and fulfilment

A passive person might blame something or someone external for what is going on in their internal world and deny their own accountability. Although rather self-defeating, it is easier to believe other people are responsible for your feelings than to accept full responsibility for your own inner state. However, doing so lifts the weight of victimhood and opens the door to new possibilities.

Taking responsibility for herself in the new circumstances reminded Lucy that she was more than a puppet on the string of unpredictable forces. Recovery remained a daunting task, with uncertain outcomes, but there was much she could do herself to improve her mental health and future prospects.

Navigate the stumbling blocks

Change can be frightening, confusing and stressful, especially if it is imposed by forces beyond your control. You may be exhausted, weary and lonely. Full of self-doubt, you may feel vulnerable and not up to the task. Your roles may have changed: made redundant at work or joining a new social circle. Your usual routines and habits may no longer be relevant, demanding you find new ways of doing things. Relationships may be very much affected, perhaps requiring you to reconsider some or establish new ones. You may encounter a myriad of difficulties that delay or hinder a smooth transition: newly closed doors, health problems, financial difficulties or relationship discord.

But you might also trip yourself up. Your expectations and attachment to certain outcomes may prevent you from being open to new and unexpected options, ideas or directions. Looking to past experience can be useful: *I did it then, I can do it again*. It can also be a stumbling block: *it didn't work then, it won't work now.* But don't be held back by past failures and seemingly impenetrable obstacles. Each situation is different; you are not who you were in the past and new problem-solving skills may be available to you now.

Don't let the unknown scare you

Most people feel apprehensive when facing a new situation. It can bring up painful emotions, especially fear of the unknown and fear of failure. You may be telling yourself scary stories about your situation and prospects, but don't be tripped up by feeling hopeless, inadequate or afraid.

Accept that uncertainty is part of your current reality and that it may push you beyond your comfort zone. If you are apprehensive, beware the following myths:

- *If I had more confidence I could do this.* Wrong. Only getting out there and being brave will strengthen your confidence: doing new things, solving problems, overcoming challenges and seizing new opportunities. And not giving up if the first attempts don't work out.

- *If I had more confidence I would not feel uncertain, apprehensive, despondent or full of self-doubt.* Not true. Those emotions pop up without invitation; don't be deterred by them. Let them be and persist even if things don't work out at first. Only by challenging yourself to step into unknown territory will you learn to cope with uncertainty and create the changes you need to make.

Accept the pace

Moving on from adversity will take time, effort and persistence.

In some cases it may be like climbing to the top of a mountain with a definite endpoint and a limited number of pathways to get there. Once there, the climber has certainty about achieving the goal.

In other cases, progress is more like crossing a desert of shifting sands. Guides or other travellers may provide information and advice for the route ahead but progress consists of meandering forward in a general direction rather than following specific routes.

Lucy's case was like crossing a desert. The general direction was clear - getting strong and healthy again - but the way to it was not defined. Realising that she could not sail through or force her way out of her current predicament, she accepted the pace with all its ups and downs was right for her now.

Some days she felt stronger but at other times she could almost not face the world. She learned to be gentle with herself and not give up in tough moments. When her thinking was muddled, she accepted that only watching TV or reading magazines was possible. On 'good' days she took the opportunity to do more normal activities. Most importantly, she drew on humour, looking for the funny side of things wherever she could. She made sure to avoid anything that would drag her down and only allowed people into her space who would lift her spirits.

No longer hating herself for who she had become, Lucy began treating herself with kindness and understanding. She still had a long way to go and perhaps would never again have quite the same seemingly unlimited resources of energy. But by managing her condition wisely - and hopefully improving it - there was no reason why it should prevent her living a satisfactory life.

Guide posts

1. Whatever your new circumstance, take it as a starting point for new beginnings.
2. Actively look for new options, solutions and pathways that are within your control.
3. Face the unknown with courage and the willingness to step beyond your comfort zone.
4. Take responsibility for your inner life - how you think about your predicament, how you deal with your emotions, your choices and actions.

Chapter 2

Calm The Body

Responses to difficult changes and traumatic incidents cover a wide range from brief stress reactions that get better by themselves to more complex and long-lasting effects.

Physical symptoms include weakness and fatigue; appetite changes; digestive upsets; aches and pains; headaches; insomnia; jaw tightening or teeth grinding; heart palpitations or irregular rhythm; reduced self-care; increased use of stimulants (such as coffee) or relaxants (such as alcohol, drugs).

Emotional effects may be frustration or irritability over small disturbances; zombie-like numbness; despair or depression; absence of hope; generalised anxiety; being prone to excessive worry; panic attacks.

Mental signs may be difficulty concentrating; making more mistakes than usual and becoming accident prone; focusing on negatives; hyper-vigilance, flash-backs, nightmares.

Spiritual effects could include feeling disconnected from life; lack of compassion for self and others; loss of faith; loss of meaning and purpose; questioning the benevolence of a higher power.

If you are experiencing several of these symptoms, it does not mean you are weak or going crazy. The shock of your experience may have unbalanced your body's operating systems and over-aroused your nervous system. In that case, strategies for self-calming are essential as they help you function in life and create a stable base for more specific mental and emotional work.

Wendy, Sue, John and Amad's story

Basic security installations and a night watchman guarded the storage and distribution facility of a large pharmaceutical company. That particular evening all the employees had left except for John and Amad who were finishing up in the warehouse, and Wendy and Sue staying back in the office to prepare an urgent job for the following day.

Suddenly, a masked armed intruder burst into the office. Sue was tied to a desk and her mouth taped to prevent her screaming. Gun in her back, Wendy was ordered to take the intruder to the warehouse where a particular drug was stored. Although a legitimate medicine prescribed by doctors, it was also a popular street drug for its mind-altering effects. Wendy did not know its exact location. Hearing unusual sounds, John and Amad came to check what was going on but were ordered to fetch the drugs. With his loot secured, the robber left. The three employees released Sue who was still tied up in the office, and called for help.

Following the incident, management took steps to upgrade security on the premises. It was generally expected that after a few days off the employees would resume their duties and return to 'normal'.

For Amad it was business as usual. He was satisfied with the support from family and friends and although he did not sleep as well as before he thought it would pass by itself.

Wendy was troubled. Previously a quiet and measured person, she was often overwhelmed by intense and volatile emotions, easily startled, irritable and prone to impulsive actions. This affected not only her work but also her private life and relationships within the family.

Sue was overcome with worries. She had felt so helpless and vulnerable during her ordeal. While tied up on her own in the office during the incident, she had begun imagining nightmare scenarios of what might be happening in the warehouse and whether she would even come out alive. But although no one was hurt that evening, she could not shake a pervading sense of unease. In her daily life too, irrespective of the situation, she imagined all sorts of disasters that might happen and began to always expect the worst outcomes.

For John it was not his first armed hold-up. In his previous job as a delivery driver for a large cigarette company, his van had been robbed by a gang, for later sale of the cigarettes on the black market. As he had for that incident, he decided to put the recent hold-up behind him and continue life as before. But then, out of the blue, he experienced a panic attack.

Unfortunately this did not remain a single occurrence. Anything reminding him of the armed hold-ups began to trigger full-blown panic attacks. It got worse, even just anticipating panic made his mouth dry, his heart race, forming a lump in his throat and pain in the chest. Was he losing his mind? He had always been such a calm and competent man but not knowing what to do with these new developments left him feeling very vulnerable, edgy and increasingly anxious.

Immediately following the incident, the company provided the affected employees with some counselling sessions and access to a GP. Psychotherapy and/or pharmaceuticals are common treatment approaches for traumatic experiences. However, contemporary science increasingly shows the effectiveness of body-centred interventions like yoga, massage and exercise and other strategies for increasing equilibrium in body, mind and emotions.

Choose from the different approaches below. If you lose your focus during any of the exercises, gently bring it back. Attention can be quite volatile. Do the exercises any time and as often as you like: when you feel out of sorts, as a daily routine, before or during a stressful situation or afterwards for calming down again. Over time the benefits for your emotions, mind and body will build up and help you navigate life with less turmoil.

Breathe

Breathing techniques are the most versatile for self-calming. Because they are done internally, you can use them anywhere and at anytime without anybody noticing.

Technique 1

- Select a word or sentence that for you symbolises relaxation such as *calm, still* or *I am at peace.*

- Sit or stand in a comfortable posture with your back straight.

With eyes open or closed, feel both feet in contact with the floor. With a few small movements relax your shoulders, chest and abdomen as well as the muscles of your mouth, jaw and throat.

- Place a hand over your navel and breathe naturally. As if a balloon is filling or deflating in your belly, your hand will rise on the in breath and lower on the out breath. With your upper body still and relaxed, keep breathing until it feels slow and rhythmic.

- With gentle breathing, silently say your chosen word for a few times as you breathe in and out. There should be no stress or gasping, just a calm flow.

- When finished, breathe normally and continue what you were doing before in a much calmer manner.

Technique 2

- Check your posture and straighten it but without getting tense.

- Feel your feet make contact with the ground.

- Notice your breathing - don't worry if it is quite shallow or rapid.

- Keep breathing but make the out breath longer than the in breath. For example, count 1-2-3 for the breath in and 1-2-3-4 for the breath out. You can also count from 1000 to 2000, whatever you find comfortable.

- Don't force anything, just count and follow the slow, gentle rhythm.

- You may notice that your breath flows deeper towards your abdomen.

Hold a posture

Assuming a specific posture will affect the flow of energy in your body. It can help unscramble your brain and soothe troubling emotional energy when you feel confused, vulnerable or upset. To settle your nerves, choose from the following exercises:

Exercise 1

- Put your right hand under your armpit near your heart.

- Put your left hand on your right shoulder.

- Stay in this posture until you feel a shift.

Exercise 2

- Put one hand on your forehead.

- Put the other hand on your chest.

- When you feel calmer: leave your hand on your chest and move the other from the forehead to the belly.

- Wait until you feel a shift.

Exercise 3, Cook's Hookup, an energy medicine technique:

- Sit down and cross your right ankle over your left.

- Extend your arms in front of you.

- Cross your right wrist over your left wrist.

- Clasp your fingers together and pull your hands underneath your arms and up to your chest.

- Rest your arms against your body with your hands at your chest.

- Take four slow, deep breaths, in through your nose, then out through your mouth.

- You can add an affirmation, for example, *I can get through this.*

Exercise 4, a simple qi gong technique:

- Lift one arm straight up. Notice how it feels.

- Move the arm to your side, palm facing downwards. Imagine a string attached to your wrist, gently raising and lowering the hand as far as is comfortable.

- Breathe in through your nose as the hand is going up, out through the mouth when going down. Make the movement slow and regular, like a pendulum.

- Pay attention to how it feels.

- If you like, use a pleasant affirmation such as *my whole body is calming down* or *I can settle my nerves ...*

Visualise

Imagery is a powerful technique to calm a stressed body and mind. If you like this approach but find it hard to visualise, try it with just holding the image as thoughts:

- Imagine a glowing sphere of light above your head. Give it a colour that you associate with peace and calm.

- Inhale the coloured light through the top of your head.

- Exhale it through every part of your body.

- Notice the soothing energies flowing through you, softening all feelings of tension.

- Think of a word that represents the feeling and say it to yourself quietly or silently.

- Later, whenever you feel tense during the day, take a breath, say or think the word and let tension go.

Calm your heart

Researchers at the Institute of HeartMath, California, demonstrated that calming the heart rate has a profound effect on body and mind. In particular the quick coherence technique synchronises the heart, brain and gut into calm and coherent rhythms:

Step 1: heart focus

Gently focus your attention on the centre of your chest. If you find it hard to imagine, place your hand on the area. If your mind wanders, bring it back to the centre each time you notice.

Step 2: heart breathing

Imagine your breath flowing in and out of the central heart area. Don't force anything, just breathe gently in and out until it feels smooth and regular.

Step 3: heart feeling

While breathing, recall a positive feeling - a time when you felt good inside, a feeling that is meaningful to you or even an emotion you would like to have. Try to experience it: joy with a beloved pet, gratitude to a family member, a fun activity. If you can't really feel something, hold the word in your mind: *gratitude, love, fun, peace.* Continue to breathe with heart focus and heart feeling.

If you have the means, the 'Inner Balance' app and sensor for mobile devices will guide you through the process and visually monitor your degree of calmness.

Wendy explored all of the above techniques and made sure

she remembered what to do when overwhelmed and upset. Her go-to exercise during the day was conscious breathing, while holding the postures was really effective in moments of acute distress. But wanting more than just relief when stressed, she added the visualisation and heart coherence strategies as meditations in her home.

First aid for panic

Following a disturbing event in a particular situation or place, the brain remembers the strong emotions felt at the time. Quick in making connections, it tends to generalise the feelings and apply them to other situations similar to the original event, giving rise to fears and somewhat superstitious beliefs about their assumed danger. This happened to John: it was not only the warehouse that could give rise to panic. Seemingly without obvious reason and when least expected, times or locations reminding him of his ordeal could also trigger an attack.

Panic attacks are extreme states of acute anxiety. Their sudden onset, intensity and unpredictability make them a terrifying and physically painful experience. Racing heart, rapid and shallow breathing, chest pain, dizziness, dry mouth, shaking, tingling and a lump in the throat are just some of the commonly experienced symptoms. They can be so overwhelming that it feels like going crazy, losing control, passing out, even dying. But ruling out underlying medical conditions, substance abuse or side effects from medications, none of the symptoms are lethal.

Even just anticipating panic can cause fear and trigger some of the symptoms. Like a fierce storm that cannot be fought or suppressed, reasoning can neither prevent nor stop an attack.

It has to be accepted as happening but can be contained with a powerful first aid strategy:

- When you feel panicky, sit down if possible (or sit up if laying in bed).
  Your head needs to be higher than your body.
  Stay in this posture.

- Focus your attention on your breathing. The aim is not to breathe deeply (a deep in breath increases hyperventilation and panic) but with a rhythm where the out breath is longer than the in breath.

- Count in your head while consciously breathing
  1000, 2000 ... in
  1000, 2000, 3000 ... out
  You can count with any numbers but make sure that the out breath is longer than the in breath.

- Take a sip of water if possible.

- Wait a few minutes. Panic may linger, but usually the worst will be over.

- Finish with a 'hookup' to support your nervous system: place the middle finger of one hand in your navel and the middle finger of the other hand in your 'third eye' (above your nose, between the eyebrows). Push in the upper finger and pull up your navel with the other finger. With eyes open or closed, breathe deeply and slowly a few times without counting.

John practised this technique in calm moments to be familiar with the steps, even writing it on a card to keep in his pocket in case he could not remember it during an attack. Taking control as soon as he noticed terror rising, John learned to steer himself through the attacks. As his fear of panic diminished he even challenged himself to go further: instead of avoiding certain places he deliberately went near them and remained until his internal storm subsided.

Contain worry

Everybody worries. But shaken by the armed hold-up, Sue's worry was out of control. Anticipating future dangers everywhere, she lived in persistent dread and began imposing restrictions on herself and her teenage children in an attempt to keep them safe. Her logical brain understood that most of the anticipated worst-case scenarios were unlikely to happen, but realism had no chance against worry.

The main problem with worry is that it does not actually *do* anything. Nothing changes for the better if you worry - not the situation, not the outcome. But worry feels important and real, as if it can prevent terrible things from happening. Determined to break the hold worry had on her, Sue used a strategy that initially struck her as very odd and unlikely to have any effect. However, desperate for relief, she tried it anyway:

At the beginning of each day decide on a time when you will worry, (at 5 pm after work, at 8 pm while the kids watch TV, whatever fits in with your lifestyle). Treat it as an appointment with yourself.

During the day, each time you find yourself worrying remember that you had allocated a special time for addressing your concerns. Write them down and decide to postpone your worries till that time and get on with whatever you are doing. You will find that difficult, especially when just beginning with the technique, as worry always seems to contain an important message that has to be believed right then and there. Persist.

Later, at the specific worry-time, review your postponed worries. You will find that quite a few have vanished. For the concerns that remain, ask questions to put them into perspective:

- *Is it a real problem or unrealistic worry?*

- *If the feared circumstance happens, what can I control or positively influence?*

- *How can I minimise problems that might occur?*

- *What is beyond my control and needs to be accepted?*

- *How can I cope with uncertainty?*

Challenge each worry in any other ways you can think of.

Sue sometimes forgot to set a time in advance and had to hastily decide on one during the day. She also did not notice each time she got caught up in worry. But the practice helped her develop more realistic ways of looking at situations and took the steam out of obsessing - to the great relief of her teenagers!

Guide posts

1. Remember that you have the power to rebalance your overwhelmed body and mind.
2. Choose from the general self-calming exercises and practise them regularly.
3. Use the specific techniques for panic and worry as first aid when needed to reduce the intensity and frequency of your symptoms.

Chapter 3

Deal With Loss And Grief

Any life-changing event involves loss. It could be through death, a relationship breakup, disillusionment with an ideology or cause, the loss associated with transition into another developmental stage of life, partial or permanent disablement or any other major change.

Within the obvious losses are other, more existential ones: the loss of the person you might have been; the loss of the life you might have lived - a dream shattered, an expectation not fulfilled, a plan stymied, a vision no longer achievable or valid. In such cases you do not only lose something, you also lose your way.

Brooke's story

It was the second anniversary of her brother's death and Brooke was inconsolable not only because of her loss but also because the whole situation remained full of uncertainties. Don had spent many years abroad living with his Asian wife and young daughter. Despite the distance, he remained close and in frequent contact with his family of origin while his wife was less interested in connection. The marriage had its problems but Don adored his daughter and was very involved in her upbringing. Then he died suddenly in somewhat mysterious circumstances.

Don's parents were shattered and so was Brooke. In conversations with Don's friends and work colleagues overseas, speculation and innuendo surfaced - that he may not have died of natural causes, that there may have been some involvement by his wife, intent on securing financial stability for herself alone. Nothing was ever proven but the family's grief was now compounded by uncertainty and suspicion.

What was the truth? Were there any warning signs they should have noticed? How could they get clarity? All of their attempts to probe further were futile. How could they find resolution without ever knowing the true fate of their beloved son and brother? The many unanswered questions only added further to the agony about the loss.

The grieving process

The grieving process can be understood in different ways. The most common one is in terms of five stages: denial, anger, bargaining, depression and acceptance. Not everybody experiences all of the emotions, or in that order. There is a great range of individual variations due to differences in personality, age, culture, spiritual or religious beliefs, quality of social supports, gender, past experiences and the complexity of the loss.

Another way of understanding the grieving process does not focus on the sequence of specific emotions but describes the process in terms of four main phases: shock, acute grief, adjusting to the loss, reinvesting and re-engaging.

Shock or numbness is a common reaction immediately after becoming aware of a loss. People in this phase typically experience a mixture of disbelief, confusion, tension, physical symptoms (feeling sick, trembling, coldness), apprehension, anger. They may also feel an unusual sense of calm, as if the world has stopped or suddenly became unreal. Usually this phase only lasts a short time until the reality of the loss hits with full force.

Acute grief is characterised by intense reactions. Waves of emotions and physical responses may fluctuate: yearning for the lost object or person, ruminating about the circumstances of the event, overwhelming sadness and despair, spasms of distress, sometimes guilt, social withdrawal, reduced functioning, confusion, intrusive dreams and memories, insomnia, loss of energy and other physical symptoms. This phase can last from days to years and can be frequently re-experienced.

Moving on from acute grief requires working through the discomfort and pain in all its wild and overwhelming intensity. Feelings need to be accepted, tolerated and faced openly and honestly. Suppressing them can result in psychological problems such as chronic depression or substance abuse.

During the adjustment phase, pain and overwhelming sorrow are transformed into more bearable and often gentle sadness. People may resume more of their normal life with a renewed sense of stability and continuity. Rather than believing all is lost, they may also begin to view their loss from a more life-affirming perspective - reflecting upon its significance, taking stock of their new circumstances and assessing their options for the future.

The final phase of reinvesting and engaging with a new life often takes a long time to develop and in some cases is even resisted. The difficulty is knowing how much is too much emotional pain and how long is too long. Other people may say: *you should be over it by now,* or worse, *snap out of it,* but timing and intensity are different for every person. It is your right to honour your experience and do things your way. Just be aware that if your emotions are turning your life toxic, reducing your options and keeping you stuck, it is time to bring some light into your inner life.

Loss can contain a transformative power - if you allow it and take steps to use it. Transforming the experience of loss into one of personal growth and discovery does not mean minimising the loss or deleting it from memory. It means accepting the event as a call to redefine yourself and build a new life. Many people discover new strengths, develop new skills and set new goals. Some also report increased closeness to loved ones, a resetting of their priorities or reinventing themselves in a way they never thought possible.

When grief is complicated

For many people, the emotions of loss - anguish, sorrow, regret, longing for that which is gone, feelings of failure or incompleteness, disillusionment, even self-pity - remain so frightening and overwhelming that the mourning process becomes severely derailed:

Absent or delayed grief: remaining in a state of shock and denial for an extended period of time, people may continue to feel emotionally numb and detached from reality.

Unusual or atypical expressions of grief: without an apparent sense of loss, some individuals become overactive, engage in risky or dangerous behaviour or make radical personal changes unrelated to the loss. Other problematic reactions involve excessive feelings of anger or guilt, the onset of anxiety, phobias or obsessive symptoms, mental preoccupations, deterioration in health habits.

Prolonged or chronic grief: extreme distress continues to be felt as acutely as when the loss had just occurred. Pain and suffering never seem to end or decrease in severity. This may eventually turn into a chronic condition with serious physical, mental, emotional and spiritual consequences.

Brooke and her family experienced complicated grief. Despite the lack of evidence a seed of doubt about Don's death had been planted and was fed by their dislike of his wife. Ruminating and obsessing about this without any chance of resolution poisoned their lives and prevented resolution. Focusing primarily on the specifics of his death, they were unable to look back at Don's life with the fondness and gratitude it deserved.

Worst of all, they had become so preoccupied with their own loss that Don's little girl was all but overlooked. The family saw her as her mother's daughter and while not rejecting her outright kept her at a distance. In reality of course, the child was also Don's daughter and had been his joy and pride. She was the major legacy of their beloved son and brother. By letting her fall by the wayside the family was in danger of losing that connection also.

Find your own way through loss

Honour your feelings

- Give yourself permission to experience and express your emotions.

- Don't be ashamed of your reactions.

- Practise self-compassion and guard against self-pity.

- Take time out if you need it.

- Keep a journal, go for walks, express yourself artistically.

- Allow moments of joy or peace - it doesn't mean you forget or dishonour what is lost.

Watch your thinking

- Avoid words like *never, always, can't, why me?*

- Practise realistic and constructive self-talk: *I am able to handle this, I can make the best of it, it is possible to make a fresh start.*

- Choose any other thoughts that might help you move forward.

Use your resources

- Accept support and share your experience.

- Stay involved and take part in normal life even if you don't feel like it.

- Allow fun and humour - lighter moments help heal wounds.

Trust in your strength and resilience

- Know that you have what it takes to cope, even if it does not feel like it at first.

- Go at your own pace.

Find the treasures

- What has not been lost?

- What have you learned about yourself?

- What new possibilities may be there?

- What will help you set a good life course?

- Imagine yourself in a new life - what has been gained?

Guide posts

1. You have the right and ability to move through loss and grief in your own way.
2. Allow healing to occur in its own time.
3. Practise the steps described in 'Find your own way through loss'.
4. Trust that from loss new life and joy can emerge.
5. If you have serious concerns about your ability to cope, consider consulting a therapist specialising in loss and grief work.

Chapter 4

Move On From Depression

It is not uncommon to experience dark moods after significant life changes. A shaken sense of self, reduced options, shattered plans and dashed hopes for the future easily open the door to feeling lost, worthless and depressed.

The word 'depression' is used for different scenarios. Some people claim it for minor problems like being disappointed, hurt or discouraged. Others use it to describe feelings of such heaviness and dejection that they are barely able to function in life.

Depression might be an inherited disposition of melancholia with occasional bouts of feeling bleak and not very hopeful. In other, more severe cases, it may be a lifelong debilitating condition requiring clinical intervention to redress chemical or hormonal imbalances within the body. The most common form, however, is depression triggered by difficult life circumstances.

Simon's story

The finance world had been good to Simon. Flying high with a good salary and lucrative commissions, he and his partner enjoyed a glamorous lifestyle: catered entertaining, expensive designer clothes, trips abroad. Money was not an issue, especially as Michelle also earned a handsome salary in a senior managerial position. Life was good.

Then the company restructured. None of the new positions matched his particular skill set and Simon became redundant. He was incredulous. How could it be that someone who had worked so hard, was respected and admired by his colleagues and valued by his superiors, was no longer wanted? Surely he should have been given a chance to adjust his skills to the new requirements instead of being thrown on the scrap heap? What he thought were reasonable expectations had come to nothing and the rejection left a deep wound. He felt betrayed, rejected and discarded through no fault of his own.

In an instant, Simon's life had changed. A generous redundancy payout softened the blow for a while but then the stress of the change took hold. He felt defeated, inadequate and worthless, enveloped by a sense of discouragement and disappointment. His sleep suffered and only alcohol seemed to dampen the pain. Smoking again after giving it up years ago, he felt exhausted, physically, mentally and emotionally. Things he had previously enjoyed no longer interested him. As if enveloped by a dense fog he lived with an overwhelming sense of sadness and futility.

In the beginning, old friends visited but it did not make him feel any better. They still had their jobs; he no longer belonged to their world. Words of encouragement and optimism that he would soon find another position sounded hollow to him. He could not see his way forward. In any case he preferred his own company now.

Stress-induced/situational depression

Simon had not previously been prone to depressive feelings but the loss of his job shattered his whole self-image. In his senior position he had been a person of importance, now he had become a nobody. Previously, his whole identity had been tied up with being the successful high-flyer - his life had revolved around it - and once that was gone, he no longer knew who he was. He was stuck and as if trying to hold on to his old self, spent hours on websites linked to financial matters as he had done in the past instead of doing something more proactive about changing his circumstances.

Stress-induced/situational depression is very much linked to external circumstances that overwhelm a person's ability to process and deal with them. There is a very strong link between severe stress and depression. Focusing on the symptoms alone will not bring about a positive shift: attention also needs to be given to the situation itself. A three-pronged approach promises the greatest chance of overcoming the mood disorder:

- Symptom relief by remaining active and engaged in life or, in severe cases, professional help and/or temporary medication.

- Depressive thinking is like travelling on well worn ski tracks in the snow, proceeding on established paths - specific neural circuits in the brain - of misery and despondency. Feelings of inadequacy are increased by inaction which in turn leads to even darker moods, resulting in a vicious circle that needs to be broken.

- Changing the situation that triggered the depression, or if that is not possible, changing the way it is viewed and handled.

Steps to recovery

Simon could only envisage future work as a replica of his previous position but that kind of job was not easy to come by. He needed to expand his narrow definition of himself and his capabilities and begin problem-solving and thinking laterally. To do this alone was not easy, however, fortunately for him, Michelle took on the role of buddy.

She understood that Simon could not just 'snap out of it'. She also refrained from giving advice, pushing him into things or jollying him along. She listened when he made comments about how he felt and gently engaged in talking with him about it. With compassion and empathy she reminded him that together they could turn his situation around and get through it. She even persuaded him to agree to an action plan:

Improve self-care. It had been weeks since Michelle had seen Simon in anything other than a tracksuit, unshaven and dishevelled. Gently coaxing him to improve the personal care he had very much neglected, she got him to have a haircut and pay more attention to how he dressed. She also made sure they ate nutritious meals and drew him into helping her with small jobs.

Use physical activities. Simon refused to go to a gym - too crowded, noisy and intense - so they took up walking, quite slowly at first but increasingly faster and for longer distances. To Simon's surprise he rather enjoyed it. They took up cycling. The movement, fresh air and nature surrounding them made them both feel more alive and optimistic about the future. They experienced what science increasingly confirms: that exercise is a powerful anti-depressant helping to improve dark moods.

Increase positive experiences. The couple realised how necessary it was to take a break from their problems and do things they enjoyed. Still emerging from his previous bleakness, Simon could not think of anything he wanted to do. But Michelle had made a list of options for him to choose from - coffee at the beach, watching a movie - just small things to get a bit of distance from the daily routine and refresh their perspective on life.

End isolation. After losing his job Simon had become quite a hermit so re-establishing social contact was essential, not only in order to re-engage with outside life, but also from a very practical perspective. If he was to ever find a new job he needed to draw on his existing network of friends and acquaintances, previous contacts and anybody who might help him with fresh ideas and options.

Stepping out was not easy. Simon could not help comparing his situation with that of other people, especially those they had previously socialised with. In the past he had been on top of the world, now he had to swallow his pride and meet them from a different position. Putting on a brave face, he accompanied Michelle to an arranged dinner. As it turned out the evening was rather pleasant, their friends were very sympathetic and Simon even got a few hints for future work.

Create new internal stories. Negative self-talk had infested Simon's mood, thoughts and actions. He realised he needed to consciously step away from negativity and develop a more positive and realistic state of mind. He began stopping himself from saying negative things about himself and his situation. He paid particular attention to words like *devastated, never, hopeless,* questioning their truth and replacing them with more realistic ones like *shaken, upset, sometimes, might need effort.*

Invoking the power of affirmations, Michelle suggested he repeat the following statements as often as possible - even have them written on a card to pull out when negativity set in:

> *I can choose my thoughts.*
> *I don't have to leave my negative brain on autopilot.*
> *I can override it to think rational and realistic thoughts.*
> *I shall focus on my strengths and the positives in my life.*
> *I believe that I have what it takes for a bright future.*
> *Even if I don't feel the energy to do something, I can choose to do it anyway.*

Get set for action. Like many depressed individuals, Simon became accustomed to using the phrase *I can't* whenever he felt helpless or disinclined. But replacing *I can't* with *I won't* puts a new spin on the situation. Correcting himself each time he said *I can't*, Simon said instead *I won't* :

> *I can't go to the shops became I won't go to the shops.*
> *I can't look for a job today became I won't look for a job today.*
> *I can't face them became I won't face them.*

Simon did not like doing this at all because it forced him to accept that he was capable but chose not to act. Just making the small change meant acknowledging that actions and thoughts were within his control. It meant admitting: *I could if I shifted a bit*. It meant admitting that he had the power to move. And it meant accepting that he had a choice. Although uncomfortable, it was rather empowering.

Replacing the word *can't* with *could* further awakened a sense of personal choice and new possibilities. For example:

I could make those phone calls.
I could shave today.
I could do the dishes.
I could look further into this job prospect.

But what about disinclination? Simon did not like being a lowly jobseeker at all. He did have the power to take action - if only he felt inclined to do so. However, not liking something is no reason not to do it. In other words, Simon did not have to like searching for work but that did not have to prevent him from doing it. This led to the thoughts: *I don't have to like what I choose or have to do. I only have to do it - whether I like it or not. It is not the end of the world to do something I don't like doing.* To Simon's surprise, facing his disinclination honestly and without being swayed by it gave him a sense of control over his emotions.

Strengthen self-esteem. To help Simon accept himself in his new situation, Michelle suggested making a list of 25 things he appreciated about himself and his life.

At first, Simon could not think of anything at all. But Michelle helped him remember personal traits like being generous, kind, supportive, well spoken, a good cook. They also added strengths relevant to a work situation: organised, team player, intelligent, strong work ethic, being considerate of others, open to learning new skills. Initially, there were a few *yes, buts* from Simon who saw admitting his strengths and positive traits as dubious self-congratulation. However, he also understood that making such a list was useful in rebalancing his negatively skewed assessment of himself and his life.

Guide posts

1. If you find yourself beset by situational depression as a result of difficult life changes, remember there is nothing substantially wrong with you. You have been thrown off-balance by challenging events and need to find new grounding.

2. Use whatever help is available - you may be surprised by how tiny blessings can lift your spirits.

3. Each day set yourself small goals, even if it is something you are disinclined to do: physical activity outdoors, talking to someone, looking after yourself.

4. Appreciate who you are and make a list of your positive qualities, strengths and the remaining positives in your life.

Chapter 5

Disarm Anger

Anger is a common reaction to the shock of unexpected and difficult events. It masks other feelings like helplessness, fear of the future, disappointment, grief, despair, regret or guilt. Anger also provides some sort of anchor for the instability and emotional volatility in the experience.

Narelle and Dee's story

Narelle had envisaged a different kind of wife for her beloved son and did not hide her disappointment. She found it hard letting go of her central role in Eric's life and could not resist offering unsolicited advice and comments on the couple's lives.

On the other hand, Dee did little to hide her dislike of her mother-in-law. But despite tense relations, Dee supported the children's contact with both their divorced grandparents. And although she did not approve of her son's choice of partner, Narelle had to admit that the marriage had no obvious difficulties and the grandchildren were well brought up.

Eric remained on close terms with his mother. She was proud of him, a strong man in the prime of his life and a high achiever in the corporate world, with all the trappings of success.

Then it happened. A freak sailing accident resulted in Eric sustaining severe and extremely serious head injuries. Prospects of his recovery were grim and the hospital doctors could not rule out lasting damage to Eric's mental abilities.

At a time when the family could have pulled together, it fell apart. On Dee's instruction no one was allowed to visit, isolating Eric from all but his own small nucleus. The relationship between the two women deteriorated. With the mother demanding access to her son and the wife restricting contact, angry and abusive text messages flew back and forth. Their relationship became increasingly toxic in a highly charged atmosphere of resentment, rage and fight for control.

Narelle and Dee's world had collapsed after Eric's accident and their response was fighting each other. Dee's aggression was likely a combination of reasons: shock, confusion and her pent-up dislike of Narelle causing her to lash out at her as an obvious target. Dee might have also feared that her mother-in-law would dominate Tom's recovery or that she could only cope with the situation by taking complete charge of the fate of her family. Narelle who tended to be over-invested in her son's life, reacted with extreme distress and fury to having her involvement curtailed by Dee, in this situation.

The high cost of anger

An outburst of anger provides a fleeting sense of empowerment and relief from emotional stress by producing unique hormones that mobilise the body. However, despite the rush of feeling strong, in control and able to handle 'danger', it rarely changes things for the better.

For people unable to let go of their anger, there will be negative effects for the immune and nervous systems, blood pressure, digestion, heart, liver, lung and other organs. It may also poison their life and well-being more generally - causing lasting damage in relationships, finances and quality of life and making them prone to dissatisfaction and frustration by everyday stressors:

- the behaviour of other people
- by association, everyone *(all men are bastards)*
- the imperfections of people *(stupid women drivers)*
- annoying family members
- people who don't do what you expect of them
- minor provocations
- arguments about sex, money, children, chores
- 'normal people' who live their life without upheaval
- people who 'don't understand'
- places, sounds, sights, smells
- people who infringe on your emotional or physical borders, treat you unfairly, manipulate, disrespect or dictate how to think and feel

- feeling inadequate or powerless

- feeling unappreciated

Choose progress over anger

If at all possible, mending the fractured family relationships within Eric's family would require a lot of goodwill from all parties. Narelle was the first to rise to the challenge and made a crucial choice. Despite considering Dee a 'bitch', she decided she would no longer engage in war. Accepting what she could not change, she redefined her priorities and resolved to focus on moving forward within the constraints of the situation. Instead of pushing or demanding, she needed to ease her way back into her son's life carefully and softly.

Narelle's new approach was helped by Eric's return to his own home. Incapable of providing all of her husband's substantial rehabilitation needs, Dee had to release her grip and relinquish some control. She was exhausted and had to consider the children. With the engagement of a professional carer, Eric's singular reliance on his wife diminished and he regained some independence for the long road ahead of him.

Narelle took advantage of the opening and seized the next opportunity for contact. Without attaching any strings or referring to current difficulties, she sent a card and gift for her grandson's birthday as she had always done in previous years. Eric responded by text, thanking her. What a breakthrough! After some weeks his doctors thought spending time on the farm with his father, Narelle's ex-husband, would aid his rehabilitation. As the former spouses remained on good terms, Narelle was informed of this development and used it for further contact with Eric on the phone, even considering a visit.

Without realising it, Narelle had begun practising essential skills of anger management.

Your anger management toolkit

Accept the reality of the situation. Making peace with 'what is' does not mean you condone what was done to you by other people or that you don't care about what happened. It also does not mean giving up in resignation. It means being very clear about the distinction between what you can control and what you can't. Fighting, raging against things you cannot change is a futile dead end. But accepting things as they are even if you do not like them or they continue to hurt you, enables you to look for new options. Then you can take action and change the things you can control.

Take responsibility for your anger. Contrary to common beliefs, no one *makes* you angry. It may seem completely counter-intuitive, but anger can only be triggered if you allow it. Letting others get under your skin gives them power over you and pushes you into a defensive role. On the other hand, not taking the bait and refusing to be pushed into angry reactions lets you be in charge of yourself. It sets you free from being bonded to the cause of your adversity and opens the door to new developments.

Know how you tick. Tune into yourself and ponder the emotions that triggered your anger. Is it hurt or fear? Shame? Self-hate? Hopelessness? Have a good look at the emotions and thoughts that fester behind your anger and intensify it. Pay special attention to blaming and accusing. If your predicament resulted from other people's actions, analyse the incident and their likely motives for what they did, even their background. It is not about excusing their action, just understanding their true role in it. Did they set out to hurt you or did it happen in the course of other events? For example, a car accident may be the result of momentary inattention by the driver. You may realise that you too had moments in the past when you only just avoided collision.

Watch the flags. What pushes your buttons? Do any in the earlier list of triggers apply to you? Write them down and decide that you don't have to hook into every problem. Think of different ways to approach your situation: with patience, understanding, conciliation, indifference, flexibility, inner stability. Remember, you don't need to be played by external factors, you can choose your own game.

As soon as you feel anger coming on - feeling hot, clenching your jaw, throbbing temples, tight stomach, voice high or loud, heart pounding - stop, look and listen. Notice what is happening with your body, posture and voice, and take action.

For rapid relief, use the HeartMath technique 'go to neutral': when you feel anger rising, shift your focus to the area around your heart. Follow your breath going in through your heart (in the centre of your chest) and going out through your solar plexus (above your navel). Breathe this way a few times. Tell yourself, *go to neutral.* Keep breathing and do not get involved in angry thoughts. If they really pull on you, keep internally repeating the sentence, *I am in neutral,* until the wave of anger subsides.

Voice your anger. Ranting and raging are rather basic forms of letting off steam. Instead communicate your anger to the person(s) involved. Calmly let them know how you feel and what their actions have done to you. It will free you from their influence.

You may even ask for an apology but if it is not possible or not provided, let it go. You don't need it for your future well-being. If the person is not accessible you can write a letter and decide whether to send it, keep or destroy it or share it with a trusted person close to you.

In some cases it may seem necessary to seek justice. But remember that the legal system does not aways deliver the result you might reasonably expect. In fact, the process may cause additional hurt. Consider if it is worth your physical, emotional and financial energy to engage in legal proceedings that may go on for a long time. Sometimes it is better to cut your losses, let bygones be bygones and move on with life.

Use imagination to let your anger go. Imagine sitting next to a creek or river. If you find visualising difficult, just think it: floating on the surface of the water are large brown autumn leaves, drifting along in the current. Tune into yourself. What are your thoughts, your feelings? Give them a name: *fury at Emma, hate for what he did to me.* Place each thought, feeling, sensation or impulse on a leaf and see it floating away.

Guide posts

1. Take a good look at your anger: is it helping or hindering your situation?
2. Address any other emotions involved.
3. Choose the anger management strategies that will help you turn the corner.

Chapter 6

Face Anxiety

Anxiety takes many forms. Generalised anxiety disorder (GAD) is a pervading sense of unease and fear often quite unrelated to particular events. More than shyness, social anxiety is an overwhelming fear of embarrassment and humiliation in social situations. Phobias attach threatening meaning to a particular circumstance or item, such as birds, stepping on cracks in the pavement or seeing a black cat. Worry and panic also share common features with all forms of anxiety:

- Preoccupation with the future or the past: dwelling on potential 'dangers' or past calamities

- Hyper-vigilance: being on the lookout for problems and painful experiences

- Feeling hopeless and powerless

- Avoidance: trying to be 'safe' by avoiding people or places, going to certain places only at certain times or only with someone else, leaving early or other coping behaviours

- Fear of the fear: where symptoms are interpreted as signs of impending calamity

- Disruption of daily life: relationships, jobs, education etc.

Diane's story

Diane was in a bad way. Leaving the house was an ordeal as she was certain that people were not only gossiping but stalking her. Especially men.

It all began some years ago. She was the only woman in a small company whose staff mostly came from the same European community as Diane and her husband. Her job in administration required frequent contact with the other employees. One of the men, Trev, fancied her but she made it quite clear that she was not interested. That was the start.

The harassment included waylaying her when she was moving through the office or warehouse, waiting for her when she came out of the toilet, sexual innuendo like singing suggestive songs, calling her *sexy woman*, whistling and looking her up and down in a demeaning way. False rumours about her conduct began circulating not only at work but also outside among members of her close-knit community.

Trev's tactics became increasingly nasty but help was not forthcoming. Diane's boss chose to ignore the harassment and even began interacting with a new - very young - female staff member in a highly flirtatious and inappropriate way. Worse still, he too indirectly demeaned her and minimised her substantial contribution to the success of his company.

Diane did not fare much better on the home front. Her husband was not generally inclined to emotional support - if he even realised that it was needed. Having kept the extent of her ordeal from him, Diane's husband was not aware of the severity of the bullying and the hurt it was causing his wife. Her father-in-law had never liked her and would not be any kind of support for Diane.

Quitting her job did not put an end to her ordeal: random phone calls with heavy breathing, a motorbike riding back and forth past her house at odd times and her standing in the community severely compromised by the innuendos. Intimidated and unsure how to deal with the situation, Diane withdrew more and more into herself. Her self-esteem plummeted, eye contact with people and especially men became difficult; attending community functions was agony. A pervading sense of unease settled in her. Believing it to be full of hostile people, the outside world became a dangerous place. Overwhelmed by a feeling of powerlessness, Diane now only left the house if she absolutely had to, but self-imposed restrictions did not ease her mind. Instead, fear began ruling her entire life.

Symptoms of anxiety

Anxiety is not only anticipation of imminent danger. It also causes symptoms on deeper levels. Physically, there may be tension, fatigue, digestive-tract problems, rapid breathing, pounding heart and others. Mental difficulties include confusion, impaired concentration and decision-making, memory problems. Emotional and spiritual effects may be irritation, moodiness, loss of confidence, discouragement, hopelessness and despair.

In her state of anxiety Diane could not sleep, was constantly on edge, hardly ate and began shaking at the slightest difficulty. When she had to leave the house she did so with an overwhelming feeling of dread, constantly scanning her surroundings and her head spinning with anxious thoughts: *what if ...* or *I bet ... is going to happen*. Fleeing from the things that triggered her fear produced a short-term reduction in anxiety but it did not resolve her internal anguish. Even as the main danger disappeared and the harassment diminished, Diane's anxiety remained.

Every person has the potential to draw on immense inner stability and strength but if the connection with the precious internal source of power is interrupted or lost during the course of life - as it was for Diane - extreme vulnerability, self-doubt and a belief in the impossibility of dealing with life's challenges take hold.

The triad of thought, feeling and action

Fear's power and pervasiveness is based on a vicious cycle of fear-based thoughts, anxious feelings and restricted behaviour. They are so interlinked that each can enhance the others and intensify distress.

Imagine a real or imagined danger like failing at something or being rejected. Your thoughts might be: *I won't get over this, I can never show my face again, I feel bad so it must be bad.* Your feelings are full of apprehension and dread with physical sensations of anxiety. Your coping behaviours consist of doing things that help you feel better or safer.

Diane felt so ill and apprehensive about having to go shopping (feeling, sensation) that she obsessed about passing out or vomiting in the supermarket aisle (thought), so she ended up not going to the shops at all but began shopping online instead (behaviour). Attending a community celebration (behaviour) triggered such anxiety symptoms (feeling, sensation) that she was sure everyone would notice (thought).

The triad is not an impenetrable gang of three. You can harness any of the three parts for overcoming anxiety.

Break the cycle

Addressing your emotions directly is difficult. For example, affirmations like *I won't panic, I won't be scared, my face will not go red* will not be effective. But you can challenge your fearful thinking about all the things that can go wrong: *I just can't face him, I will lose the promotion, they'll never invite me again*. Replace it with more realistic thoughts: *I can do this even if I feel afraid, I can tolerate anxious feelings, I am capable of figuring out what to do if something goes wrong*.

The most successful way of liberating yourself is facing the fear and taking action anyway. Of course, if there is the possibility of real danger - such as after leaving an abusive situation - take decisive action to prevent harm. For less extreme scenarios use a strategy of gradual exposure as outlined below:

Begin with a small step into a feared situation just beyond your comfort zone and stay until your anxiety has peaked and receded. You may feel flat or exhausted afterwards. Next time, stay a bit longer or add another difficulty. As you increase your exposure to what frightens you, you will come to realise that you can take charge and that anxiety does not have to consume you.

For example, if you are terrified of being in public places, begin by going to a quiet coffeeshop and only stay a short while at first. The next time stay a bit longer, each time increasing your stay, even adding other difficulties like speaking to strangers. Stay with your feelings until the grip of fear diminishes. If you had a car accident at a certain corner but cannot avoid the place indefinitely, stand well away on the footpath and wait until the fierce dread subsides. Next time, take the difficulty up a notch by walking along the edge. Continue challenging yourself step by step until you feel ready to try driving there again.

Overcoming anxiety is not easy and may take a long time but the shift from weakness to strength is guaranteed if you persist. It does not mean you will be free forever from feeling fragile and anxious. However, instead of going into a downward spiral of fear when that happens you will be able to take charge and decide what action to take.

Remember that you are stronger and more capable than fear will have you believe. If action is needed to get out of the way of danger, take it. If anxiety blows threats out of proportion or creates imaginary scary scenarios, face them and do not be swayed.

Decide who is in charge - you or your anxiety? Take back your power, one small step at a time!

Guide posts

1. Recognise the triggers for your anxiety.
2. Take stock of your avoidance behaviours.
3. Challenge your anxious thoughts and replace them with realistic and life-affirming ones.
4. Accept your feelings of fear but do not let them stop you.
5. Make a plan for gradual exposure to a situation that causes you anxiety.

Chapter 7

Check The Stories You Tell Yourself

Everybody has their own repertoire of ongoing automatic monologues: judging, making assumptions about the feelings and motivations of others, predicting outcomes, commenting, interpreting and evaluating events. Such internal storytelling is a powerful tool to make sense of experiences and resolve issues.

However, when life is difficult the mind's default setting is to highlight negatives, tell scary stories, dredge up painful memories from the past or predict future calamities. The inner chatter becomes far from accurate and full of all-or-nothing thinking, catastrophising, overgeneralising or jumping to negative conclusions with statements like *all is lost, my life is finished, I will never recover from this, I won't trust anybody ever again, I am a total failure.*

On the other hand, self-supporting stories are about *I can.* They are not about sugar coating an experience or 'thinking positive'. In fact, if positive affirmations are not in alignment with your underlying beliefs, they will be ineffective until the belief has been revised. For example, you may be telling yourself *I am powerful* but if your deeper belief is *nothing ever works out for me* your affirmation will have no effect and you may get even more despondent than you were in the beginning.

Evan's story

His new relationship with Nikki going well, life could be a relatively smooth ride - if only Evan could resolve the custody issues involving his two young sons. After two failed marriages, with a son from each, he was still dealing with the fallout from the breakups.

Custody for his first son was shared, while the second wife gained sole custody of their baby son. His problems with pornography and recreational marijuana were seen as compromising his ability to be a good role model for the children.

Having successfully overcome his addictions, Evan increased his efforts to be included in his sons' lives but in a strange twist the two ex-wives developed a close friendship and appeared to be sabotaging his attempts at contact: arrangements for visits were changed or cancelled at a moment's notice, phone calls to his sons blocked, messages not relayed.

Evan imagined the worst scenarios of being alienated from his sons, of being rejected and missing out on all the important events and milestones in their lives. He was at a loss about how to make peace with the women and assert his rights as biological father.

In two minds

Evan's own father died when he was only a few months old and his mother remarried. Life was difficult. His older sisters resented having to babysit or take him along to their own activities. They even went as far as tying him to a tree when meeting their friends and walking away from his pleas for release and inclusion.

Evan's two failed marriages bore similarities to his upbringing. He had hoped for loving and supportive relationships but sabotaged this by recreating a subconscious pattern: a difficult family life with a troubled young man and women who undermined rather than supported him. Something he was not aware of drove his choices and actions.

The conscious mind is the seat of cognitive functions including logical thinking, planning, decision-making and problem-solving. It has the ability for self-reflection (observing and thinking about yourself) and self-determination (making deliberate choices about the direction of your life and your own being).

In contrast, the subconscious mind is the repository of programs stemming from individual predispositions as well as learned experiences. In the course of your life, people in positions of authority teach you directly or indirectly what is 'truth' or 'normal'. Once such 'truths' solidify as your own truths they become hardwired into your brain as core beliefs you hold about yourself, other people and the world overall.

Unfortunately, in cases where the acquired truths are inaccurate or wrong the brain's inner programming will repeat the same response patterns even when they are no longer relevant and create a self-defeating mechanism.

The placebo effect

Given their major differences it may seem there is a chasm between the conscious and subconscious minds that cannot be bridged but this is not the case. The two minds are interdependent to an astonishing degree.

Testing new medicines often involves administering active substances to one group while a control group receives seemingly the same kind of medication but without any active ingredients. Participants in the study do not know which group they have been assigned to. Surprisingly, patients often get better irrespective of the group they are in. The healing effect occurred with the sugar pill as if it had been the real medication. How is that possible?

The so-called placebo effect is based on participants anticipating benefits from what they believed to be real medication. This impacted the body on a subconscious level and set physical processes in motion that led to improvement in the patients' conditions.

A similar effect is associated with the so-called nocebo effect where the body also synchs with the belief to the detriment of the person. For example, people who are diagnosed with a serious illness may accept devastating prospects for recovery and survival as absolute truth. Believing themselves to be powerless their life often proceeds with limited options.

Henry Ford described this great power of the mind: *'If you believe you can or if you believe you can't ... you are right'*.

In the medical world, the mind's ability for self-healing is often judged inferior to the power of pharmaceuticals or surgery. In a psychological context though, it has major implications for change and empowerment.

Beliefs create reality

The core beliefs hidden within your subconscious act like filters on a camera through which you view life. They impact every aspect of your life and determine your truth, your perspectives on events, choices and actions. Core beliefs also form your self-portrait: how you see yourself, your flaws, strengths and potentials and your relationship to the world.

However, core beliefs are more than just filters. They are active energies of immense influence. In a subconscious process they energetically draw into your life, situations and people that confirm the beliefs you hold about yourself and others. Judging by his history, Evan's core beliefs may have been:

- *There is something fundamentally wrong with me.*

- *If people knew the truth about me, they would reject me.*

- *I always make bad decisions.*

- *I am not lovable.*

- *I am not worthy of a truly loving relationship.*

- *I don't deserve love.*

- *Women are dominant and controlling.*

- *I am powerless against them.*

With such self-defeating beliefs in his own unworthiness and shortcomings, it is not surprising that Evan attracted the kind of partners into his life who would sooner or later confirm his views of himself, women and relationships.

Identify your beliefs

It is very difficult to identify your own core beliefs. Deeply hidden in the subconscious, they are so ingrained in how you tick and so much part of your everyday functioning that they easily evade detection and continue to negatively affect your life, for example:

- Self-sabotaging beliefs relating to the value you place on yourself: *I am worthless, I am not important, I am a failure, I am a bad person ...*

- Your beliefs in autonomy: *I need others to help me make up my mind, I'll fall apart if I'm alone, I don't know how to take care of myself ...*

- Your sense of security: *the world is a dangerous place, I can't protect myself, I can't cope when things go wrong ...*

- Evaluating your performance: *I am stupid, I can't get anything right, nobody will like what I do, I have no options, I will be rejected unless I do everything perfectly ...*

- Judging your relationships: *people are not trustworthy, people are not fair, it's best not to ask for help, it will only be used against me, I don't fit in anywhere, no-one will like me, people are not interested in what I have to say, people don't care about me, I am not like them, people always leave me, nobody will want me ...*

This list is by no means complete. You could add categories like appearance *(I am ugly)*, future prospects *(nothing ever works out for me)*, parenting *(I wouldn't know how to handle kids)*, creativity *(I can never come up with anything interesting or unusual)* or any other area of life important to you.

If you find it difficult to recognise your own beliefs in such a direct way, try a more indirect approach:

Identify your rules. Core beliefs set the 'rules' for your behaviour in life in order to avoid negative consequences. They determine how you live, your attitudes, choices and behaviour.

For example, you may be very guarded in the information you disclose about yourself and keep sensitive things about your life secret. You may also be careful about believing what others tell you, perhaps suspecting ulterior motives or hidden agendas. The rules behind your behaviour are about not opening yourself up to others, showing no vulnerability, being sceptical. And behind those rules may be beliefs like *people can't be trusted* or *I can't be hurt if I don't let people close to me.*

Your rules are also very obvious in how you think and what you tell yourself: *I should, I shouldn't* (who says?), *I need to be ...* (where does that rule come from?), *I am ..., I can't* (who is the judge?), *if I don't do ... I'll be ....* (how did you learn to think in terms of cause and negative effect?). Ask yourself, *what belief or expectation may be setting the rules here?*

Recognise the patterns. Like Evan, you may be experiencing the same difficulties over and over again: different partner, same kind of relationship, different situation, same problem. Whenever you find recurring problems in your life, they are likely sustained by self-defeating core beliefs. Be the detective in your own life: review the situations and look for a common theme in them. Ask yourself, *what pattern am I re-enacting time and time again?*

Rewrite your beliefs

Make a 'greatest hits' list of your own problematic beliefs. Put them into groups if they follow a theme but deal with each one separately.

Examine the evidence:

- *Is the belief absolutely true?*

- *How did I come to have this belief?*

- *What is its origin?*

- *What was the situation?*

- *Is the belief still relevant to the person I am now and the life I wish to live?*

- *What benefit would I gain if I gave it up?*

Once you have examined and challenged your existing belief, think of a more realistic statement. When Evan did this work it looked like this:

Old belief: *Women are dominant and controlling.*

Old rules: *I have to accept a life partner who does not value me and always wants things done her way. If I don't accept this I won't have anybody at all.*

New belief: *Some women are dominant but there are also many others who are cooperative and open to communication.*

New rules: *I don't have to accept a woman who does not treat me well. It's better to keep looking until I find one with whom I can discuss things and arrive at decisions together. I will aim for a real positive partnership.*

Act as if your new beliefs are true

For real change, analysis is not enough. You also need to manifest the new belief in your life. If you find that difficult or it seems false, remember the saying: *'If you can't make it, fake it'!* Practise being the person you want to be even if at first it doesn't feel like you at all.

Once he became aware of the beliefs and rules affecting his life, Evan developed a whole new program for his current situation:

- Relationship with Nikki: meeting Nikki had given Evan hope that a different relationship dynamic might be possible for him. With her agreement it was decided to take matters slowly and cautiously, to focus on maintaining open and honest communication and making sure their relationship evolved in a mutually beneficial way.

- Interactions with ex-wives: Evan determined not to engage in fights and arguments, not complain or criticise, but only focus on increasing access to the boys. He also tried to show that he had changed and could be a good role model for the children.

- Contact with his sons: despite the limitations, there were possibilities to maintain a presence in their lives and make them aware of their importance for him. Evan made a list of small steps he could take, for example offer to babysit, take them to the doctor, attend a school function, reach out via letters, emails, messages, gifts and so on.

- Self-development: Evan was prepared to honestly face his shortcomings and failings. Instead of self-condemnation, he learned to accept his past and forgive himself for what he had done and what could not be changed. Now it was up to him to do everything in his power to manage his life differently.

Such a structured program may not be relevant or not appeal to you. If that is the case, consider a visualisation technique.

Your subconscious mind does not distinguish between actual experience or dreams and fantasies. Creating a new reality in your mind can be accepted as your new truth by the subconscious.

Sit or lay down in a quiet place where you won't be disturbed. Identify specific experiences from your early life that contributed to the negative core beliefs you now hold. Then visualise (imagine or think) your adult self visiting your inner child during those times. Being older and with more life experience you are able to view the events from a different perspective. Guide your younger self to let go of pain and the false truths imparted to it then. Like the parent or friend you needed at the time, reframe the old belief with a more accurate and positive version.

Whatever advice or support you give your younger self in your imagination will be processed and stored by your subconscious mind as if it really happened. You may have to repeat the process or get help in order to rewrite core beliefs. But while the events of the past cannot be changed, the beliefs formed at the time and the stories you tell yourself about them can.

Tame your runaway thoughts

Most people believe thoughts, words, self-talk, ideas, attitudes and assumptions as if they are facts but they are not realities. They are simply habits of mind. No matter how convincing, thinking or telling yourself something does not make it true.

It is futile to argue or fight with automatic thoughts. They have a life of their own and you have no direct control to stop them. However, it is possible to render them ineffective. The weapon is your attention!

Focus is the most potent power of the mind. Ancient Hawaiian philosophy has the saying: *'Energy goes where attention flows'.*

What you focus on receives your energy. Not getting caught up in your thoughts will starve them of energy and loosen the grip of automatic negative thinking. Use the strategy below to change dysfunctional automatic thinking into realistic and proactive thoughts.

1. Become aware of your thoughts. When you notice some of your intrusive thoughts, don't try to repress them. Just be aware of what is going on in your mind and describe it to yourself. Notice how you feel when having the thoughts. You might recognise that your thinking is going round in circles, with similar thoughts rising to prominence again and again. It can actually be quite boring to be thinking the same things over and over, like a broken record.

2. Don't fight your thoughts - change your focus. Unhook yourself from the thoughts. Be like a witness rather than engaging with them. Let them be but move your attention to a neutral place, for example, tune into yourself. Follow the rhythm of your breathing and feel your feet make contact with the ground. Become aware of your surroundings, shapes, sounds, smells, noises. Focus on the task at hand.

Experience yourself as the calm conscious presence you are. You are not running away from your negative thoughts or trying to suppress them. You let them be as if they were just white noise in the background while consciously engaging in whatever you choose to do. Imagine a small child crying: trying to soothe it, the mother tells it not to cry but the crying promptly gets louder. Noticing a puppy walking past, the crying stops. What happened? The child's attention shifted to a different focus.

It's just like that with automatic thoughts. Shifting your focus away from them and putting your attention where you choose removes the energetic hold and puts you in charge of your mind.

3. Find new thoughts that are more factual. If your thoughts are dragging you down, you need to examine and challenge them: draw two columns on a sheet of paper. On one side make a list of your negative thoughts and on the other write a realistic substitution.

When Evan used this process, he asked himself: *what is the evidence for this thought? Is there another possibility? What would be a more factual way of looking at it? What is the reality of the situation?*

Guide posts

1. Your perspectives and the stories you tell yourself are based on your beliefs.
2. Recognise the dysfunctional patterns in your life and the beliefs behind them.
3. Use your attention to change habitual ways of thinking.

Chapter 8

Upgrade Your Relationship With Yourself

The development of self-acceptance, resilience and a sense of self-worth depends on many influences. If they are demeaning, include rejection, put-downs or indifference, the scene is set for a troubled relationship with yourself and makes you prone to connect with people and situations that will treat you with a lack of respect and care.

Jeanie's story

It had all begun so well. Taken by a friend to a lecture about personal development, Jeanie was amazed at the enormous number of people attending. It was a time when many young people became followers of various spiritual teachers or gurus.

Although Jeanie had never felt drawn to such practice, she did have dreams of liberating herself from old dysfunctional patterns in herself and becoming a stronger person.

When the lecture began, Jeanie was intrigued and reassured by what seemed to be very down-to-earth and sensible teaching, plain talk and beautiful music. It was enough for Jeanie and her friend to subsequently join a group for more intensive inner work.

Jeanie had recently gone through major life-changes and was very unsure and lonely in her new life. Engaging with the group would meet many of her needs: to become the best person she could be, to belong to a community of like-minded people and find new purpose in life. Most other members were professionals who attended meetings but otherwise continued to live their normal life. Jeanie, however, gladly accepted the invitation by the leaders to settle nearby and work full time at the centre.

Honoured to have such a special position, she did not mind putting her own professional progress on hold and contributing her not inconsiderable talents and abilities for the benefit of all. But the reality soon dampened her optimism.

Social interaction and conversations were to be kept to a minimum and contact outside the society was forbidden. Without pre-existing connections outside the society, it made for a rather isolated existence. Jeanie was allocated mainly subservient jobs but the 'privilege' of cleaning and cooking in the leader's house and being drawn into their family blinded her to the sinister web forming around her.

Study groups and other activities at the centre were designed to expose the character flaws and deficiencies of the participants so they could develop more desirable qualities. However, in Jeanie's case the excessive focus on what was wrong with her and the lack of opportunity for positive self-expression was used to systematically erode her self-esteem.

The will of the leader was paramount. Without realising it, Jeanie began to censor herself and adopted mannerisms she thought pleasing to the leader: how she walked, talked and interacted with others and even the thoughts she allowed herself to have. Denying her own perceptions, intuitions and truths, her real self became so suppressed that it was increasingly superimposed by a kind of pseudo-self she thought she should be.

Holding on to her idealistic notions of self-improvement, Jeanie did not recognise the cultic nature of the society. Skilful manipulation, pervasive mental/emotional abuse and involvement in degrading activities administered in the name of psychological progress trapped her in a nightmare of terror and anguish. Finally, her despair became so great that she needed to take action if she was to save herself. Although she would be utterly alone and had to start her life all over again, leaving the society had become less frightening than remaining and losing herself completely.

How the self gets lost

How is it possible for a person to become so compliant and crushed? Why do people not simply leave at the first sign of intense control or abuse?

Idealism, romantic attachment, loneliness, expectations of a better future or simply naivety and unhappiness with life draw people into the web of abusers. Jeanie's spirit was broken within a high-control, toxic group, but similar mental, emotional, physical or sexual abuse also occurs in families and one-on-one romantic relationships.

Abusers are masters at establishing or exploiting an

imbalance of power through claiming superior knowledge, more resources, financial security, social status, love and belonging, charisma or popularity. Promising something of value only they can deliver encourages subordination of the victim.

Whatever the scenario, it always begins with a honeymoon period where the expectations of the novice/partner are validated. Life is good, the bond is strengthened and the unequal power dynamic seems acceptable. Gradually difficult incidents creep in. But as they are moderated by 'good' periods, the victim learns to accept and even excuse them as justified because of something they did or didn't do.

Rewards and punishment depend on compliance and performance: as long she does what pleases him, problems are averted - until her next (so-called) transgression. Limiting outside involvement, cutting off support, censoring social connections, preventing or reducing financial independence and dictating lifestyle further isolate the victim and intensify dependence.

Perpetrators do not take responsibility for their actions. They make light of what they did and blame the victim instead. Worn down by accusations, a person eventually accepts and learns to believe that whatever is being done to them is their fault. With a destabilised sense of self, the victim begins to believe that any chance of well-being - and perhaps survival - depends on suppressing who they are, how they think and behave. They no longer have their own self to operate from.

A word of warning. If you recognise yourself or someone else's situation in any of the above descriptions, seek help as soon as possible. Be very careful how you proceed: withdrawing from an abusive situation can be a most dangerous and vulnerable period. Abusers have extreme and often violent reactions to losing their power. Make sure you do it as safely, and with as much support, as possible.

Know your inner critic

Even with less extreme influences, most people live with an inner critic who points out faults and flaws, dwells on the negative and often is downright abusive.

Self-criticism

- Overly critical and dissatisfied with yourself
- Judging yourself negatively: *I am hopeless, I am so stupid*
- Being full of self-condemnation
- Comparing yourself to others who seem superior in some way

Self-doubt

- Taunting yourself: *not capable, experienced or good enough ...*
- Diminishing yourself: *it's only me, I know it's not very good ...*
- Finding it hard to make decisions
- Needing excessive assurance from others

Self-recrimination

- Reprimanding yourself: *how did I get into this situation? I should have known better ...*
- Results from a sense of failure, guilt or regret

Self-neglect

- Indifference or denial of your own needs

- Dismissing or ignoring your aspirations and dreams

Self-rejection, self-loathing or self-hate

- Ranging from vague feelings of low self-worth to severe self-hatred

- Expressed in extreme ways: destructive and dangerous behaviours, self-harm, suicide

- Associating with negative people who drag you down

- Sabotaging chances at peace and happiness

Shame

- This is not necessarily due to having done something wrong and being ashamed of it.

- It is the sense that there is something fundamentally wrong with you as a person, that you are worthless to the core: *if people saw the real me they would reject me, I am not okay as I am.*

- It is 'knowing' that in your very essence you are flawed.

- Shame is the master of toxic self-evaluation and poisons everything you do. You connect with people who (also) do not value you. You tolerate severe disrespect, humiliation, neglect and abuse. After all, you do not deserve better. You keep yourself small and hide your light. Success, joy or love would create unbearable dissonance with the beliefs underlying shame so you sabotage yourself in every possible way. But worst of all, it blinds you to the beautiful soul you are in your essence.

Nurture yourself

How do you transform abusive self-evaluation into a nurturing relationship with yourself? Begin by noticing how you treat yourself:

Nurturing	Abusive
encouraging	demeaning
fair	unfair
supportive	disempowering
compassionate	cruel
realistic	negative
proactive	undermining
confidence	insecure
attentive	destructive
hopeful	depressing
empathic	critical

Are you correct in your appraisal? Where did you learn to think about yourself in that way? Who made you believe it? Imagine what a supportive friend would say to you and replace your inner critic with a realistic and more positive appraisal.

In the beginning of her new life, Jeanie's pain and disorientation was so great that she chose to use 'acknowledgements'. Different to affirmations, they are statements that acknowledge something you did well that day.

Every day Jeanie reflected on how the day went. For whatever she did, thought, felt or noticed that day, she formulated three acknowledgements in the present tense. For example: *today I acknowledge myself for making a list of tasks I have to do, I acknowledge myself for not staying indoors all day, I acknowledge myself for facing my fear of crowds and going to the shops.*

Doing this exercise was quite painful at first: Jeanie was not used to looking at herself in such a positive way and felt as if she was doing something forbidden or wrong. Just finding something seemed really hard but she realised the power of this method to disable self-sabotaging attitudes and help her develop a more accepting evaluation of herself.

Find self-compassion

Adversity often brings with it hurt or harm. Feelings of self-pity are quite normal and understandable: life has changed and often not for the better. But if self-pity takes over and you don't rein it in, it is a very problematic emotion. Your perception narrows to seeing only loss, damage and problems and reinforcing the sense of being a victim.

Unlike self-pity, self-compassion is not about feeling sorry for yourself, blaming others or dwelling on misery. It appreciates the difficulties of your situation and your inadequacies without getting lost in self-recrimination.

Remember that being human brings with it vulnerability and imperfection. Accept your shortcomings and realise that all you can ever do is what you are capable of at any given time. You deserve to treat yourself in a compassionate way with kindness, caring and comfort. Practise self-compassion by applying the steps below:

- Acknowledge your current state and formulate a statement to express it, for example, *This is a moment of suffering, I'm having a really hard time right now. It's painful for me to feel what I am feeling. This is very difficult.*

- Express a self-compassionate intention, for example, *I accept myself just as I am, I treat myself with kindness, understanding and gentleness, I endure this pain with grace, I am strong, safe and able to protect myself, I forgive myself, I find peace in my heart, I accept the circumstances of my life and live with ease and well-being, I am wise and change what I can.*

- Choose the statements you resonate with - or find your own - and combine them into a mantra, for example, t*his situation is so difficult, I can only try to do my best.*

- Put your hand on your heart or hug yourself.

- Calm your breathing.

- Say your mantra as often as needed to soothe your distress.

Self-compassion is an essential component of self-acceptance. Self-esteem mainly looks at the positive side, the inner critic only at the negatives but we are both, light and shadow. Self-acceptance knows the whole picture, all the marvellous and special qualities you have and all those that live in the shadows.

To strengthen self-acceptance, pledge that you will deal with yourself in ways that are fair, understanding, encouraging, comforting, helpful, supportive, attentive to your needs, productive and proactive, realistic and hopeful. Look within for comfort and strength and the self-compassion you need to get through your challenge.

Write your story

Jeanie felt the need to really understand her experience: why she had allowed it to happen and the effect it had on herself and her life. She wanted to do this work in private and in her own time. Processing her past would open the doors to hidden pain but one of the many techniques for self-soothing and processing described in chapters 2 and 12 would help her deal with overwhelming emotions. Another option was to say a self-compassion mantra, for example, t*his pain is almost too much to bear. I did not deserve to be treated in such a destructive way. I now love myself as the tender and beautiful person I am.*

If you decide to write your own story, use the following steps:

1. Commit to writing

- Choose a time and place where you will not be disturbed
- Begin with at least 15 minutes for a few consecutive days

2. Choose what to write

Your intention is to take a really good look at what is going on inside yourself in relation to your past or in your present:

- Your deepest emotions and thoughts, your fears and hopes.
- The facts of what happened.
- Something that is really troubling you.
- Something you have been avoiding.
- Something you cannot deal with.
- Really let go and explore your true feelings - everything you can find: their origins, reasons, difficulties they caused in your life and so on.

3. How to write

- If you are unable to write, speak into a recorder.

- You could write as if it's a conversation with yourself or any other way you feel comfortable with.

- Don't censor yourself.

- Write without worrying about grammar or spelling.

- Remember that the purpose of writing is to bring all your pain and difficulties into the light. Be completely honest with yourself.

- Name your emotions: *I feel shattered because ..., I was so scared that ...*

- Use words of insight: *I assume, realise, understand, know ...*

4. What to do with your writing

- You are writing for yourself so you can keep it private or share it with others. Some people keep their journal and then check in after some time to assess how they have changed.

- Other people use it as reference for a life story or memoir they later publish.

- Some destroy their writing in ways meaningful to them, for example, by creating their own ceremony in the backyard and burning the work with the intention to hand their problems over to the universe.

- Whatever feels right and brings you a sense of closure, do it.

5. An optional step

- When the cloud lifts and you feel ready, contemplate what you gained from your experience.

- If it is not yet apparent don't force it. Sometimes the treasures of an experience become evident only much later.

Guide posts

1. Reflect on what made you doubt and deny yourself.
2. Get to know your inner critic.
3. Nurture yourself with self-compassion and self-care.

Chapter 9

Stand Your Ground

A physical boundary is the border separating what is yours from that of others, the fence around your house, the hedge in your garden, walls around your room, your skin. It gives you the right to determine how, when and by whom you are touched or who comes into your space.

From a psychological perspective, boundaries are the mental, emotional, spiritual or relational limits on who and what kind of influences you accept into your life. They determine how you want or deserve to be treated.

Interlinked with the psychological boundaries are invisible (to perception by the five senses) layers of electro-magnetic energies. They have been described in many religious traditions as aura and in modern science as biofield. Like an energetic spacesuit in the form of an upright egg, it surrounds the physical body and acts as an important interface between your own energies and those of others.

When boundaries are trespassed by the thoughtless or intrusive actions of others it is called a boundary violation. A lack of respect, threats or attacks, ignoring someone else's rights, behaving inappropriately or going against another person's will are just some of the ways in which boundaries are transgressed.

Boundaries are not set in stone and can be flexible, depending on the situation and person involved. What is acceptable in one case and with one person may not be tolerated generally, for example, people in abusive relationships accept behaviours that others find abhorrent. Not everybody has the same boundaries: personal history, perceptions and concerns all influence what is considered safe and appropriate interaction with others.

Mike and Sarah's story

Retirement was good. Mike and Sarah had recently stopped working in their full-time jobs. Mike continued doing some private consultancy work but kept it part time. Sarah met up with old friends, spent time at the gym and thought of doing art classes. The couple very much enjoyed being able to do whatever they wanted whenever it suited them.

One day Erin, their eldest daughter, asked if she could come and stay for a while with her two young children. Erin often had difficulties managing her life, holding down a job or maintaining stable relationships. Mike and Sarah had always been very protective of her, much more than they were with their younger daughter. Now they were willing to provide her with the support she needed.

At the back of the house was a large space for Erin and the children to move into. Mike and Sarah loved their grandchildren and looked forward to having them around. They were also glad to give their daughter a stable base. Her latest relationship had failed and she quit her job as well. She did not seem able to find something that would suit and interest her and settle with it. She could perhaps take up some study, but she was unsure about what to do.

The children were excited to have Grandpa and Grandma so close. Coming home from school they talked about their little adventures and Mike especially cherished the connection. However, other things were not going as well as Mike and Sarah had hoped. There was the cooking and housework. Sarah had to take care of everything while Erin did not seem to realise - or was unwilling - to do some of the chores.

Small irritating things began piling up. Despite being asked to open them after use, Erin left the bathroom windows closed so mould began building up on the walls. She also used Mike's office and computer whenever she wanted, leaving his systems disturbed when finished. Then one day, as Mike and Sarah returned home, they saw that Erin had rearranged their pictures on the walls and shifted furniture in the lounge and dining rooms.

Sarah was livid. The ongoing upheaval in their lives created too much stress. She and Mike loved their daughter and empathised with her difficulties. Asking Erin to leave was out of the question - she was there to stay for as long as she wanted but they were no longer willing to remain passive while their lives were turned upside down. Something had to change.

The cost of weak boundaries

Easily overwhelmed and ultra-sensitive, people with weak boundaries often feel 'swallowed up', suffocated or even invaded by the moods and energies of other people. The interface between them and others is so diffuse and blurred that their energies merge indiscriminately with those outside of themselves.

Not feeling contained as their own individual selves, they are lacking a strong sense of what is right or wrong for them. They are easily influenced and often defer to the other person rather than expressing their own opinions or wishes. Low in confidence, they feel unworthy or afraid to assert themselves. Pleasing and complying with others seem the only options, but this often results in being taken advantage of or thwarted in pursuing their own interests.

For fear of being seen as authoritarian and upsetting their relationship with their daughter, Mike and Sarah asserted their boundaries with practical measures rather than direct confrontation. Mike installed a lock on his office door and fixed the bathroom window so it could no longer be shut completely. Sarah rearranged pictures and furniture as they had always been and left dishes in the sink after meals.

All this was meant to send a signal but Erin remained blind to the message. The parents finally realised that nothing much would change in the house unless they stepped up and faced the potential risks of disapproval, withdrawal of love or limited involvement with the grandchildren.

Resolve conflict

Conflict occurs when two parties have opposing ideas, interests, agendas, goals, aims or plans. Often this leads to dredging up the past, recrimination, criticising, blaming, complaining, nagging, threatening and even punishing. When emotions are highly charged, things are said that often lead to regret later on.

Resolving conflict is not always a smooth process, however, taking a win/win approach may restore peace:

- Be willing to resolve the conflict.

- Support equal engagement in the process rather than one party dominating the other.

- Recognise that not only your own point of view is valid but that the other party's view may also have validity.

- Try to understand their perspective, underlying needs, values, objectives and visions.

- Know your needs and rights and communicate them assertively if needed.

- Manage your own emotions and avoid being triggered by those of your opponent.

- Decide to be flexible.

- Look for possibilities of cooperation and mutual gain in the situation.

- Reframe the conflict: rather than as a damaging crisis, see it as an opportunity for change.

- Consider different options and brainstorm potential resolutions.

- Work towards new balances, agreements and contracts.

Sometimes your efforts at resolving a conflict may not be met with equal commitment by the other party. They may try to overpower you, remain rigid and inflexible, insist on their point of view, fight for their rights, dig their heels in or go through the motions without any intention to compromise. Recognise when this happens, cut your losses and look for different ways of solving your problems.

Cope with criticism

Nobody likes to be criticised as criticism points out imperfections, mistakes and failures. You may feel judged, wrong, guilty or afraid. Some people try to avoid criticism by being extra nice, over-achieving or by insisting they are right. Others counteract criticism more forcefully: *how dare he?, they have no right, who does she think she is?*

If the person being criticised has vulnerabilities and weak boundaries it doesn't matter if the criticism comes from someone of no importance in their life who is without expertise on the subject or bends the truth with malicious intent. It will hurt and harm as intended.

Criticism only loses its sting when we have strong boundaries and accept our own shadow side. Everybody is at some point tired, distracted, in a hurry, feeling unwell or unmotivated, misinformed and not on top of things. There is no way any of us can live without making mistakes or being less than our best.

When you are being criticised, keep a check on your own reactions of anger, defensiveness, easy agreement or defeat. Honestly and rationally assess the criticism. Is it 'playing the ball' or 'playing the man'? If the criticism gives you feedback on something you did - deadline not met, anniversary forgotten - be sure you know exactly what the issue is. Is the criticism constructive and valid? Parts of it may not be accurate or be over-stated. Disregard what does not really apply to you. Are there parts that will help you improve? Ask for further clarification if needed. Accept what is appropriate, use it for your own learning and development and take whatever action is needed for improvement.

If the criticism is a personal attack, irrational, hostile or even abusive, it usually contains generalisations and global statements like *never, always, everybody, I always have to get you out of a mess, you never ..., you can't be trusted, nobody is as stupid as you.* Even if you are in the wrong or feel bad about a situation, reject being called names or being intimidated, threatened or violated. Make your position clear, for example, *I am prepared to consider the point you are making but I will not tolerate your shouting or denigrating comments.*

If this falls on deaf ears walk away and take time out. Be warned though, that meeting abusive criticism with calmness, not engaging in controversy or turning away may well infuriate the other person further. Make sure you are safe.

Just say 'no'

Declining a request or not joining in with others when expected show that you are your own person with preferences and needs that are just as valid as those of others and that your own well-being is important. Use the following steps as a rough guide.

1. Acknowledge the other person's needs. If the request is rather general, like helping to set up the room, ask for more details. It indicates that you are considering the request but need more information before making a commitment.

2. State your position. Name your preference, feeling or perception of the circumstances. Be tactful, confident and assertive, not apologetic: *I am too tired tonight; I won't be able to lift anything with my bad back; I have a previous engagement; I'd rather not get involved; I'm too busy with my own things.*

3. Say *no.* If you find it too hard to say a straight out *no,* try these milder alternatives: *I'd rather not; I don't think it's right for me; I need to think about this one; I will be in touch if I can.*

Be assertive

Neither aggressive nor submissive behaviours create lasting harmonious relationships. Aggression is characterised by forceful demands, threats or actual harm in order to overpower the other person and achieve compliance. The other extreme - non-assertive behaviour - is also problematic. It involves deference and submission, allowing the agenda of the other person to dominate.

Assertiveness means standing up for your rights, feelings, beliefs and needs while also respecting those of the other person. It is a respectful form of communication that provides another person with a clear and unambiguous message about where you stand. It also signals a willingness for rational discussion of contentious issues.

The key to assertiveness is being polite, direct, clear and non-attacking. It might involve a straight posture, eye contact, speaking neither too softly nor too loud, keeping feelings calm, and an air of confidence - even if you do not feel it inside!

Effective assertion statements should be quite short and as succinct as possible. There is no one-size-fits-all formula for assertiveness, however, the basic 'recipe' below captures its essence and can be very effective:

1. *When you ...*

Describe the other person's behaviour, only one specific difficulty at a time. State the facts: lay your issue/grievance/problem on the table for discussion. Keep the description as factual and objective as possible and avoid interpreting the other's behaviour. For example, Mike and Sarah could have said to Erin: *When you changed the arrangement of pictures in our lounge room ...,* or *When you mixed up the files on my desk ...*

2. *I feel ...*

Without blame, intimidation or demands let the other person know how their behaviour has affected you. Mike and Sarah's example: *We felt disrespected, I felt angry and upset.*

3. *Because ...*

Give a brief description of the effect that person's behaviour had on you. Describe only observable consequences without generalisations or accusations. In Mike and Sarah's case: *Because our favourite paintings are now at the back where the light is not good ...,* or *Because I have to start over sorting my papers when you have mixed them up ...*

4. *I want ...*

Explain what you want changed. Make a request, asking only for different behaviour but not a change in attitude or values: *We want you to treat us with more respect,* or *I want you to change your attitude towards us* are too general and not descriptive enough. The statement has to be specific and describe something observable: *We want you to not change things in the house without running it by us first,* or *I want you to check in with me before using my office.*

Put together, Mike and Sarah's assertion statement looked like this: *When you rearrange the pictures in the lounge room without asking if it would be okay with us we feel disrespected and upset, because now our favourites are barely visible in the back. In future, we want you to check in with us first before making major changes in the house.*

An ineffective statement would have been: *When you hurt our feelings by changing all the pictures on the walls, we feel our house is no longer our own and you have always done things like that and upset us. We want you to respect us more.* This message is unclear, contains blame and drags up past transgressions.

In their conversation, Mike and Sarah gave their daughter loving reassurance that she was welcome to live in their house for as long as she and the grandchildren needed a home. Mike even proposed creating a separate entrance for Erin's space and generally improving it for her needs. Sarah added that as a full member of the household Erin had to share responsibilities, take on some of the chores and respect the way they wanted to live their lives.

Much to the couple's surprise, the conversation went well. Relieved to have certainty about her place in the house, Erin made an effort to appreciate their position. Her rights and obligations were clearly spelt out and agreement reached about how to cohabit in a way suitable for all. What a relief!

But the couple's work was not finished. Even though Erin had committed to change, she sometimes fell back into her old ways. They had to be consistent and not let the issue drift. Unless they insisted on the arrangements, Erin might not to take them seriously and disregard their wishes.

Being able to express yourself assertively is a very important skill. Take time to learn the 'formula' and practise for different scenarios. Perhaps role-play with a friend or by yourself in front of a mirror. Look at situations where you do (or did) not stand up for yourself and formulate an assertion statement. You need to be familiar and at ease with expressing yourself assertively so you know what to do when your boundaries are violated. However, it is still your choice whether or not to respond: not every battle needs to be fought. Sometimes walking away is just as effective.

Negotiate

Everyday life is full of negotiation. You may need to argue your case, review arrangements or present yourself in the best possible light. A general roadmap might give you some pointers.

Prepare

- Know exactly what you want: *I want a trial period before committing, I want Sue to look after Bobby for a week.*

- Make a plan for presenting your case. Decide what to say and how to say it. Key points, choice of words and body language all affect how your argument will come across.

- Think carefully about what arguments the other person may find convincing.

- Pick your time and place.

During the discussion

- Stick to the subject. Don't be distracted, waylaid or blocked.

- Listen carefully to what the other person is saying. Try to really understand what they mean, where they are coming from and what their concerns and preconceptions are. Listen to the other person's objections. Don't interrupt or argue; instead ask, gather information, clarify. But if the other person is so caught up in their own thoughts or doesn't want to hear what is being said they might argue and push back. Under such circumstances it is best to paraphrase their response in a brief sentence so they know they are being listened to.

- Make a proposal taking into consideration the other person's position.

- Ask for a counterproposal. If your suggestion is not acceptable, encourage the other person to come up with a different solution. Keep calm and don't be tempted into an argument.

- Switch back and forth listening, clarifying, proposing until both agree on a solution.

- Find other angles if the talk is going round and round in circles: suggest a compromise or point out new options.

Acknowledge the outcome

- Appreciate that you and the other person have collaboratively worked on a problem.

- If no solution was found, the difference of opinion has to be accepted. To resolve an ingrained stalemate may take time and involve alternative ways of coming to an agreement.

Guide posts

1. Reflect on the boundaries you need to set in your own circumstances.
2. Practise the steps of assertive communication.
3. Learn to say '*no*'.
4. Practise conflict resolution and negotiation.

Chapter 10

Create Your Own Change

If you have to adjust to an insignificant change you might be able to go with the flow, but if you are faced with a serious upheaval of your previous conditions you need to step up and develop your own path forward. Creating your own change within the new circumstances requires making choices and decisions, knowing what you want or need to do, determining the right timing and conditions, setting realistic goals, making a detailed plan and keeping yourself on track.

Amanda's story

It just wasn't working for her: lonely, bored and increasingly melancholic, Amanda no longer cared about the beautiful countryside. A few years ago, at Tom's urging, Amanda and her husband had relocated to the country and now lived in a charming but isolated homestead. It was his dream rather than hers, but Tom had painted such a convincing picture of how they would live a peaceful life away from the city, that she agreed.

Unfortunately reality did not match the dream. Tom's business had to be in the city and it was therefore practical for him to stay there during the week. On weekends, when they could enjoy their new life in the country together, Tom spent most of the time glued to his computer. For Amanda it was loneliness without Tom, and loneliness with Tom.

It was not what she had envisaged for herself. Amanda missed the stimulation of her previous job and the company of people - including her husband's who had become so engrossed in his own interests that there seemed to be no space for her in his life. Looking after the big house and sizeable property did not make her feel fulfilled, especially as she had accepted but not chosen the new lifestyle.

Finding the situation increasingly unbearable, Amanda suggested they move closer to the township with more manageable land and a smaller house. But Tom would not hear of it. He liked the peace and quiet on the weekends and their current arrangements suited him well. Amanda was stuck - or was she?

Be proactive

For Tom, life had not actually changed very much. Apart from increased commuting he still lived life on his own terms. It was Amanda who had to bear most of the new conditions and it was affecting her well-being and mental health.

Used to complying with her husband's wishes, Amanda had

become quite passive and found it hard to make her voice heard. In fact, while she could usually pinpoint what she did not like and what was not working for her, she was often unsure about what she herself wanted. She knew she was very unhappy in the current arrangement but was not clear on what to do about it. However, her husband's evasiveness and insensitivity to her plight woke her up. Amanda realised that only by taking action would it be possible to change Tom's attitude and her circumstances. She had to step up and take the initiative for improving her situation.

Amanda began looking for houses in the township by herself without Tom knowing about it. She needed space to clarify her own wishes and needs. She also knew she had to build a definite case and present him with concrete alternatives as only that would force him to deal with the issues and give valid reasons for rejecting her wishes. Changing her circumstances was so important to Amanda that even the dread of eventually having to confront her husband did not deter her. She had enough of being miserable!

Make decisions

If there are a multitude of different options to choose from, begin by assessing the potentials for change. Ask yourself:

- What do I need to accept about the situation?
- What can I influence?
- What are my options?
- What actions might be possible?

Once you have an overview of your situation, use the steps below to explore your options in greater detail. Don't be put off by the seemingly complicated process, it is really very simple once you get the hang of it and start thinking along those lines:

1. Formulate your question. If you need to decide between two options it's relatively straightforward: do A or B? If you are dealing with a more complicated difficulty, break it down into its components.

For example, Amanda's issues were: *What positive steps could she take? What kind of house was she going to look for? How to keep her house-hunting secret? If she found a place suitable for them both, how would she present her case to Tom?*

In steps 2, 3 and 4 Amanda explored only one of these questions at a time. Then she repeated steps 2, 3 and 4 for each of the others separately.

2. Brainstorm options. Make a list and write down whatever comes into your head. Remember to only work on one question. Keep an open mind and consider everything and anything you could do, whether or not it seems realistic or practical.

Amanda made a list of features she wanted in a new home. Some were essential, others desirable. She was careful not to evaluate, compare or dismiss anything at this stage and simply added each new idea to her list in no particular order.

3. Reduce the list. When finished, eliminate the unworkable ideas or those beyond your control but make sure not to rule out options that seem impossible now which may contain a seed of possibility for the future.

4. Assess the consequences. On a separate page draw three columns. Write your remaining options into the first. The other two have the headings: 'now/ very soon/ short term' and 'in the future/long term'. Going down your list, ask yourself for each option: *What are the consequences in the short or long term if I choose this option?* Be very clear that you are assessing the consequences, not the pros and cons.

Write your thoughts about the potential consequences into the appropriate column. You may find that something comes with short-term benefits but questionable value in the long run or a particular option seems favourable in the long term but has many pitfalls right now.

With the list of features she wanted in a new house, Amanda considered the consequences as far as Tom was concerned, for example a small block of land. In the short term Tom might reject the idea, as he saw himself as a rural landowner. In the long term it might suit him to have less maintenance and spend less money on the upkeep.

Amanda then repeated this step for every other option in the first column.

5. Make your decision. Sometimes the best solutions seem to 'emerge' from the pages. When it comes to analysing and evaluating what they have written, people often find it easy to make their decision. Just looking at the consequences of a choice lets the right one stand out but if it is not immediately obvious what course of action to take, compare the options and weigh up their short and long-term consequences. Then decide which ones are more acceptable - or less painful.

Repeat steps 2, 3, 4 and 5 for any of your other questions from step 1.

Regarding her list of features in a new residence, Amanda marked those that would definitely please Tom and those she found essential for herself. She did not cross out desirable ones but turned her main focus to the essentials.

The detailed descriptions above may give the impression of a drawn-out and confusing process. However, after applying it a few times many people move on from the formal process. Instead, weighing up the consequences of potential options becomes a way of looking at things.

Boost your motivation

Making a decision to do something is only a first step. Your next challenge is bridging the gap between intention and action. Despite your best intentions you may be very disinclined to make the necessary effort. How can you find and strengthen the necessary motivation?

One way is to envision your ideal life from a higher vantage point. What would you like your future to include? Organise your ideas into the categories below or make your own. For each heading ask yourself: *What do I want in my ideal future life?* For example:

- Your Self: feeling good, confident, self-esteem ...

- Lifestyle: freedom of choice, peace ...

- Home and Family: living with whom, where, repairing or enjoying relationships ...

- Social Life: friends, hobbies, communication ...

- Work or study: what kind, satisfying, purpose ...

- Health: free from the after-effects of the past experience, sufficient energy to do ...

- Spirituality: instruction, practice, like-minded companions ...

Beware of attitudes that sabotage motivation: resignation and expecting positive developments to be out of your reach. Many things will be possible in some form in the future. Remind yourself of the big picture and contemplate why you want to do it and what you would gain from it.

There is no secret ingredient in motivation - it is a simple cost-and-benefit formula: only when the gain from taking action is greater and more important than not taking action will you actually do anything.

Formulate your goal

In order to have any chance of success, a goal has to be specific and clearly defined. In Amanda's case, general ideas like wanting to live in a better place were too vague. She needed to be much more specific about the kind of house she wanted, the location, garden and so on. To crystallise her ideas further, she used the format for formulating a SMART goal:

Specific: *what is my exact goal?*
Measurable*: how will I measure my progress?*
Attractive: *why do I want to succeed?*
Realistic: *is the goal achievable? What useful resources, strengths, skills or previous experience can help me? Which areas do I need to work on?*
Time-bound: *what is my timeframe for achieving my goal - when and how to start, how often to review my progress, making revisions, when to finish?*

Make a practical plan

Whatever your goal, keep your plan simple and set achievable steps no matter how small. For example, make a to-do list and prioritise the actions on it. Start with the easiest and work your way towards the more difficult ones or start with the most important and leave the least important until last - if by then it still seems relevant.

Amanda became quite methodical in her approach and felt empowered by her newfound focus and initiative. She made sure to include a measure of accountability by confiding in a close friend and checking in with her regularly at specific times. She also kept a record of what she had done, what worked and what needed revision.

Plans often fall by the wayside so you get despondent, consider yourself a failure and might even give up altogether. But don't take your non-compliance as a personal failure. If your plan did not keep you on track, it's not you who failed but the plan. It just wasn't the kind of plan you would follow. Review and learn from it about yourself and the conditions you are dealing with. Then formulate new action steps that might be more do-able.

Your action plan should not be set in stone. You might be going in one direction but encounter all sorts of obstacles. Sometimes the road to achieving your goal is not as straightfor-ward as assumed. Be flexible and creative in navigating road-blocks and detours rather than letting them stop you. Review what you are doing and what is working for you. Don't lose sight of your goal and look for new ways of getting there. In fact, sometimes a detour is full of learning and the real change occurs along the way.

To sustain your own efforts, confidence and positive outlook, give yourself credit for even small achievements. Be proud of any small step forward no matter how slow or insignificant it may seem. Beware the opinions and comments of other people unless they are supportive. Only you know what you are facing and the changes you have to make.

What is there to help you?

What guidance and information is there to find out what you need to know and point you in the right direction? Who might support you with affection, affirmation, frank appraisal or aid? What are your own resources? Are you underestimating your own skills, strengths, resilience, determination, flexibility and wisdom? Is your glass half full or half empty?

Once you look closely, you will find you have many useful skills. But if specific ones are not relevant, assess your transferrable skills. For example, a housewife with children has skills in time management, budgeting, conflict resolution, organisation, food preparation, cleaning, the social arena. Make a list of your own skills.

Your strengths are also a potent resource. They often overlap with skills but are not the same: creativity, leadership, teamwork, curiosity, love of learning, open-mindedness, flexibility, determination and persistence, social intelligence, fairness, humour, self-control and vitality all fall into this category.

To find your strengths, consider what you are good at and what you might develop further. If needed, get additional input from someone who knows you well. This is not the time for unnecessary humility or fear of aggrandisement. Be realistic and practical.

In time you may choose to develop new skills and strengths to go into a completely different direction than in the past but reminding yourself that you are a competent person rather than seeing yourself as powerless and lacking anything to build on will help you make a start right now.

What trips you up?

Fears, flaws and failure: is your mind often tuned in to Radio Triple F? Are you glued to the scary stories inside your mind? What is that doing for your motivation, get-up-and-go and rational thinking? Making changes will be full of uncertainty, rattled confidence, mis-steps and fears. But Radio Triple F is the wrong station to listen to: it will sabotage your best efforts and fuel self-doubt.

It's not just a matter of switching off the station, you have to understand why you are attuned to its messages. Shine a light on your own triple Fs. Where do they stem from? When did they start? How did they develop? Was love and acceptance dependent on you doing everything 'right'? Have you been forced by circumstance to do things you have no natural talent for? Ask your own questions to find out what is driving your fears, fixation on flaws and anticipation of failure. Dig deep to find what is holding you back.

Perfectionism is a real roadblock to progress. Perfectionists are experts at focusing on fears, real and imagined flaws and anticipated failures. In case you suspect such tendencies within yourself, check if any of these characteristics apply to you:

- poor judgment of when details matter and when the big picture is all that counts
- difficulties delegating
- fearing repercussions for anything less than a very high standard

- horrified by failure or mistakes

- afraid of being exposed as being 'imperfect', having weaknesses and showing vulnerability

Even if you try to do your best, sometimes it just may be less than perfect. This should not stop you from having a realistic but compassionate attitude towards yourself and developing the best version of life you are capable of. Don't allow negative expectations to deter you, instead choose to have courage and trust that new things are possible even if there are hiccups along the way.

If your resolve to move forward weakens, remember that things rarely improve by themselves, fear does not disappear by avoiding stressful situations, you only avoid feeling it and confidence does not magically appear from somewhere. Be brave and do not be deterred from making your own changes.

A special tip for changing yourself

External change often demands that we also change. In many cases such change occurs gradually just by dealing with the challenges but you can also intentionally manifest change in yourself with the following meditation.

At a time when you can be quiet and undisturbed, sit or lie comfortably, perhaps with a candle burning and meditative music.

Search within yourself for a sense of who you want to be. Imagine or just think about that person. In your mind, visualise or think of yourself living, being and behaving as that person. What will you be saying to yourself, how will you feel? Imagine (or think about) many aspects of that future You. Create that new person in your mind. Make it as real as you can, as if it already exists.

As you come to the end, decide on a symbol representing that new You. Some people choose an animal, others choose a colour or object. Find something that has meaning for you. Use your symbol in whichever way you find helpful. For example, put up a picture, write a story about what it means to you, remind yourself of it whenever you feel a bit shaky. Use it as your own guide post to the future You!

Guide posts

1. Assess your options and make decisions about how to proceed.
2. Formulate SMART goals and make a realistic action plan.
3. Consider your resources for change.
4. Reflect on potential obstacles and setbacks.
5. Make sure to boost your motivation.

Part 2

Thrive

Chapter 11

Make Peace With The Past

Memories are like symbols of experiences rather than exact records. When an event is recorded as a memory, it goes through your own emotional and cognitive filters, assumptions, interpretations and perhaps even embellishments. This is one of the reasons why several people can have quite different recollections of an event they all witnessed.

Memories are not fixed. Like video and audio recordings they can be modified, enhanced, played louder or softer, rearranged and edited with special effects added, reissued in new versions. They may also diminish or recede into the background as time goes on.

Why memories hurt

As records, memories are not a great problem; it is the emotional charge of a memory that makes it so potent. For example, events that do not invoke strong emotions - passing people in the street - do not create strong memories. But if an event involves pain, distress, anger, love, excitement or other intense feelings, the memory and the emotions associated with it will be stored together. That is one of the reasons for people's pain and upset many years after an event when they remember what happened.

The emotional charge of a memory comes mostly from the stories we tell ourselves about the experience. Consider two very different stories about the same event. Accepting an event in a matter-of-fact way, one person might say: w*ell, it happened and although it was anything but pleasant, I can't do much about it. Better get on with things and deal with the new situation.* Another person on the opposite end of the spectrum might say: *it's a catastrophe, I'm totally devastated and will never recover from this, ever.*

What effect will their memories have on their lives? Which person will pick up the pieces and move forward, which one will be stuck in the past and miss out on the opportunities for a new life? If the event was significant neither of the two people will likely forget what happened but for one person it will be the factual record of a difficult time while for the other it will be an emotionally charged memory that retains its power.

You cannot change history and the record of it remains but you can change the energy of a memory by facing the emotions associated with it and changing the stories you tell yourself about the event.

When memories are suppressed

There was a man
who was so disturbed
by the sight of his own shadow
and so displeased with his own footsteps
that he determined to get rid of both.
The method he hit upon was to run away from them.
So he got up and ran.
But every time he put his foot down
there was another step,
while his shadow kept up with him
without the slightest difficulty.
He attributed his failure
to the fact that he was not running fast enough.
So he ran faster and faster, without stopping.
Until he finally dropped dead.
He failed to realise
that if he merely stepped into the shade, his shadow would
vanish,
and if he sat down and stayed still, there would be no more
footsteps.
Poem by the ancient Chinese sage Chuang-tzu (369-286 BC)

How does this relate to memories? Consider its message about avoidance. Postponing to face something painful can be useful. It is sensible to take charge of your own rate of progress, even it means switching off temporarily. Perhaps you have heard someone say: *I can't deal with this right now,* or *I am not ready to face it.* Some people need time to get into the right headspace before they can deal with serious matters but when avoidance becomes ingrained or maintained by self-destructive behaviours, urgent action is required to prevent further harm.

The poem above also contains wisdom about dealing with painful memories. '*Stepping into the shade*' means facing the emotional darkness, staying and shining a light on the memory until the emotional energy dissipates.

Disarm your memories

A word of warning. The following self-help strategies may not be appropriate in cases of severe trauma, abuse or PTSD (post-traumatic stress disorder). Be mindful of your inner state. Discomfort and suffering may be inevitable, but if you fall into a pit of such despair that you cannot find a way out, do not continue without help. Enlist a person close to you or a therapist to support and assist when your own coping abilities are overwhelmed.

If you choose to proceed, do so at a time and in a place that allow privacy without distractions. Some people go to a particular place to relive the event while working to resolve their recollection of it. Others tuck themselves away in a private corner. Do it your way whatever that is. Proceed at a pace comfortable to you, with stops and starts as you need them.

Work with the body. In this technique you are not addressing the memory and its emotional charge directly but working on them indirectly through the body. You are not trying to change your recollection but change your body's reaction to it.

When you are settled, recall the memory. Feel the place in your body where you are most affected. Hold your attention there and let it soften. Gently breathe into it, continuing until the tension or feeling recede. When one part feels better, again tune into the memory and find another place where it affects your body. Repeat as many times as needed. The process will be complete when you can recall the memory calmly or it now seems far away.

Watch a movie of the event. This strategy uses imagination and visualisation. If you find that difficult, do it as thoughts. Make sure you are in a place where you feel comfortable and safe, perhaps with a person close to you.

Close your eyes and imagine (think) watching yourself in a movie. See (think) yourself as if performing on a screen, safe and okay before the traumatic experience. Then start a film of the event as you remember it. See what happened, how you and other people acted and anything else that deeply affected you.

You might cry or feel other intense emotions. Let them be but don't get drawn into them. Just sit and watch it all unfold on screen. At the end, imagine (think) the film being rewound at very fast speed to the safe starting point and return to the time when you were your old self. Let your emotions settle and realise the event has not destroyed everything. You may be different to how you were before the experience but you are okay. There still is life right now and ahead of you.

Write the story. This strategy which was described in chapter 8, works well for memory work. The writing will anchor you and help you not disappear into your pain. It also provides a vehicle for expressing your emotions.

Forgiveness - a gift to yourself

The idea of forgiveness makes many people shout *never!* Indeed, it seems completely illogical to contemplate forgiveness for someone who has caused you significant hurt or harm: *I'll never forgive him for what he did, it's unforgivable how she behaved.* Resentment, blame, recrimination and desire for revenge seem so much more natural than forgiveness. Is there anything to be gained by forgiving an offender?

Formerly associated only with spiritual well-being, it is now known that forgiveness enhances emotional, mental and physical health. It is also a way to make peace with the past. Releasing hatred and bitterness breaks the troubling connection with the offender. No longer consumed by what was done to you, you can move beyond the offence. Without the crippling emotions, wounding can turn into wisdom and understanding. You will then be able to learn from the experience and come out the other end a stronger, better person.

In essence, forgiveness is about asserting your strength and resilience for your own good. It will not make you look weak or vulnerable and it does not mean you are condoning what happened or minimising the offence. In fact, if possible and appropriate you can clearly express the impact the harmful actions had on you. Your forgiveness does not depend on the offender deserving it, asking for it or expressing remorse. If there is no sign of change or sincere regret there is no need for reconciling.

Ideas that block forgiveness

- *What happened is unforgivable.* No matter how despicable the action was, your mental health will improve if you release the emotional charge and accept the incident as a time in your past you can leave behind.

- *The offender is all bad, he must pay.* If you decide that action is required to protect yourself or society, or to stop them re-offending, take the necessary steps. But pursue justice with a clear head rather than emotional entrapment.

- *I need to wait for the offender to change or see the error of her ways.* Your forgiveness does not require anything from the perpetrator. If you see signs of regret or making amends it's a bonus but you should focus on healing yourself, not the offender.

- *I'll betray myself if I let anger, resentment and blame go.* Hanging on to the feelings gives them energy and allows you to be controlled by them.

- *I don't need to forgive. I'll make myself so strong and invulnerable that no one can hurt me.* But what sort of life is it with walls around you, suspicion of others, always on guard for fear of being hurt? Forgiveness frees you to build trust in yourself that you can handle whatever life presents you with.

- *If I forgive and let go, I'll have to take responsibility for my own happiness and well-being.* Blame is easier but taking the reins of your own life is infinitely better than remaining chained to the past.

Are you ready to forgive?

Forgiveness is commonly understood as a benevolent emotion towards the offender but you might not ever be able to feel that and it is not necessary. There is a different kind of forgiveness that does not require turning hurt into positive feelings. This is based on a matter-of-fact acknowledgement of the events where you understand how it came about and each person's part in it.

In that kind of forgiveness the once overwhelming emotional charge is replaced with indifference or neutral acceptance of what happened. Bondage to that person is released by withdrawing from the victim/offender dynamic. Letting go of suffering takes the offender to 'zero' where they no longer play an influential role in your present and future life.

Forgiveness is a choice you can make or not make. You may never be ready or be ready only many years after the incident. Do it in your own time. You might consider forgiveness when you:

- are willing to let the past be past

- are prepared to look at the incident rationally and from a broad perspective, taking all factors into account

- are tired of feeling like a victim

- accept that it's up to you to liberate yourself

- realise that no one but you can take your pain away

- want to move beyond negative self-talk to more constructive and positive thoughts

- question the idea that a past offence is responsible for your present unhappiness

Practise forgiveness

Forgiving is a difficult process that may take time, effort and determination. Progress is rarely smooth, often by two steps forward, one step back with surges of strong feelings. To process the experience work in private or with a trusted person and include at least some of the following steps.

1. Tell the story. Your story needs to be expressed and heard - even if only by yourself. Choose the form you are most comfortable with: through writing, artistic expression, imagination or any other way. Describe what happened. Clearly identify the person(s) who caused you harm. Acknowledge that an offence has taken place and assign responsibility appropriately.

2. Process the hurt. Face and validate your feelings: they may rise and subside, fluctuate, getting stronger or weaker, overwhelming or dying down. Hang in there with mindful awareness until they recede. Challenge your thoughts connected with the feelings. Are they rational or dramatising the situation? Are they true and realistic or merely insistent? Are they making you feel worse or helping your emotional release? Remember your ultimate aim - to lift the emotional clouds within you and free yourself from the negativity that keeps you tied to the past.

3. Investigate the story. Be open to move from judging to understanding. Why might the other person have behaved the way they did? What is their story? Was the offence intentionally directed at you or was it a result of their own failing? Did they set out to hurt you or were you in the wrong place at the wrong time?

4. Tell the story differently. Use your new perspective to reframe the experience with greater understanding and detachment.

5. Integrate the shift. One way is writing a forgiveness letter to the offender. You can send it but it is not necessary to do this: forgiveness is about you, not them. It is about confirming your newfound attitude, whether it is based on compassion or indifference. Keep the letter, burn it or release it to the universe, whatever gives you a sense of completion. Another approach is to create a ritual that symbolises your shift, for example, choose an image or words meaningful to you and draw it onto a balloon. Release it into the sky with the intention of freeing yourself from the negative emotional ties.

Acknowledge your new perspective to yourself or a person close to you. And don't forget to be grateful that you had the strength and courage to extend forgiveness to someone who may or may not deserve it. That no longer matters - the most important part is achieving your own inner freedom.

Update on Jeanie's story (chapter 8)

Sometimes it is easier to forgive the actions of another person than it is to forgive your own transgression or mistake but there is no benefit to self-condemnation. It carries guilt and regret from the past into your present and future without changing anything.

After her experience in the cultic group Jeanie was haunted by her past, full of shame that she did not recognise the truth earlier, that she allowed herself to be so easily manipulated, forsaking her own values and aspirations. Jeanie was riddled with self-recrimination and regrets about her involvement: *I should have seen it coming, I knew better but still did it, if only I had not been so ... It's all my fault, I can never forgive myself.*

In order to not let the experience define her for the rest of her life, Jeanie had to release the burden of regret and guilt and forgive herself. This required looking at the events, her actions and her mindset at the time, in a non-judgmental way.

Processing the experience. Facing the truth of her own involvement and acknowledging her own shortcoming was very painful. Many times Jeanie had gone against her better judgment and strong intuition. It was all part of her blind submissiveness and misguided loyalty to the leaders. She had engaged in activities she was not proud of but now she did not flinch from admitting the hurt her actions caused herself and others. It was essential for her well-being to get to the truth so she bravely tolerated her discomfort until new understanding emerged.

Finding a new perspective. Jeanie was not condoning what she did or neglected to do; instead, she looked at her part in the situation from a different perspective. She realised that like everyone else she was a flawed and fallible human being who did not deserve self-imposed negativity.

Instead of judging herself, Jeanie tried to understand why she did what she did. She reflected on her reasons for joining, her childhood experiences and programming, why she had fallen under the spell of an abuser to the detriment of her own happiness and well-being. Although it turned out so badly she had done the best she could with the knowledge she had in the circumstances at that time. Accepting this, she was able to look at herself with compassionate eyes.

Integrating the shift. Jeanie realised her shortcomings were not the total sum of her being. She was damaged and had made grave mistakes but she still had many positive qualities. What happened was one period in her life that she could move on from and start over. Consolidating her new attitude of self-acceptance, Jeanie wrote a forgiveness letter to herself and created a ritual that symbolically released her self-condemnation.

It did not happen overnight but after much inner work Jeanie was able to view her time in the group, its leaders and herself with a degree of neutrality instead of anger, regret and self-recrimination. Relieved of the emotional charge of her memory, real transformation could take place. As time went on she was able to build a productive and satisfying life for herself. Some physical damage remained but she was now emotionally detached enough to manage what could not be repaired, with pragmatism and acceptance.

Fear, shame and self-hate no longer ruled Jeanie. She became a better and wiser person with more compassion for herself and others. In fact, her experience changed her whole outlook on life. She no longer sweated the small stuff or accepted things at face value. Beginning life with a very underdeveloped sense of self, extremely low self-worth and very weak boundaries, she became a person with self-awareness, inner strength and self-love.

Guide posts

1. Forgiving does not condone what happened.
2. If you are the one who transgressed, let go of self-condemnation.
3. Forgiveness is about releasing the emotional bondage to the event.
4. It is not about replacing hurt with warm fuzzy feelings. Neutral acceptance of the event, taking the offender to 'zero' provide the same kind of freedom from the past.
5. Allow the idea that forgiveness has nothing to do with the offender deserving it but is based on the understanding that no one is perfect.

Chapter 12

Create Emotional Stability

It is useful to think of emotion, body and brain as a triad where none of its parts acts completely independently of the others. Activity in one area will inevitably affect the others. A wave of emotion usually does not last very long and would diminish by itself if our minds did not get involved. It is thoughts and self-talk that amplify them into a prominent place in our attention until we are all consumed by them.

For example, if we are upset about something our distress usually worsens the more we think about it. We might also get physical symptoms like feeling quite sick in the stomach or beginning to shake. Negative emotions have adverse effects on our hormone-, cardiovascular- and immune systems, digestive organs and metabolism. But if the body feels good, our mood lifts and worries are temporarily forgotten.

You can manage your energies by harnessing any part of the triad to effect change in the other two. For example, a regular relaxation practice will calm the mind and emotions. Choosing rational thoughts will settle the body and soothe emotions. Letting emotions run their course without getting hooked into them will quieten thoughts and soften the body.

Ride out emotional storms

Feelings come in waves, often appearing out of the blue, and are triggered by a memory, words overheard, pictures or experiences. The more we are trying to rein them in, suppress or ignore them the stronger and more persistent they get. To have any chance of control, they need to be witnessed and allowed to diminish in their own time.

Imagine yourself rowing a little boat when a storm begins to form. You are aware of the fierceness of the wind and the choppy pulse of the waves. There is no point wrestling with the storm, it will take its own course. You may feel unable to cope but if you give up you might drown. Your best chance of not being swamped is to stay calm, be conscious of what you are dealing with, keep rowing and manoeuvre your little boat through the choppy sea until the storm subsides and you reach calmer waters.

Working with emotions is just like that. It requires you not to shy away from feeling the emotion, no matter how overwhelming it seems at the time. Like rowing your little boat through a storm, you remain present while it is raging until the feeling gives way to a calmer state.

Use the strategy below while in the grip of an upsetting

feeling, for emotional storms or - when you are less overwhelmed - for looking into a specific emotion that keeps interfering with your life and well-being.

1. Prepare

- Find a place where you won't be disturbed.

- Sit comfortably and breathe, making the out breath slightly longer than the in breath.

- Feel your feet solidly on the ground.

- Bring to mind the troubling emotion.

- Keep breathing.

2. Face the emotion

- Become aware of the feeling and name or describe it to yourself.

- Ask yourself: *what is this feeling? What is going on here? Where in the body do I feel it? What is this about? Do I know this feeling? Have I felt it before? In what circumstance?*

3. Accept your feeling

- This does not mean just putting up with the emotion while getting more and more tense and waiting with clenched teeth for the storm to subside. It means letting the body loosen as much as possible while accepting that the emotion is there and you are experiencing it.

- Breathe and stay present to whatever you feel no matter how frightening or overwhelming.

- Do not shrink away from the feeling.

- Say to yourself: *it's okay to feel this way, I am okay, I won't die.*

- Keep breathing.

- Stay and let be whatever is.

4. Float through

- Don't fight with the emotion or yourself for feeling it.

- Don't struggle or force anything.

- The emotion does its thing and you do yours.

- You coexist; there is no need to get involved in its drama.

- Let yourself float through the emotional waves.

5. Persist

- Full recovery from emotional turmoil may take a while.

- To get the full benefit from the exercise it may have to be repeated many times and for other emotions as well.

- The body needs to learn how to rebalance and settle.

- Old habits of your mind are not easily shifted and even if it seemed that a particular feeling was resolved once and for all, it might pop up later for no particular reason. In that case, don't get upset but practise facing, accepting and floating until it passes.

6. Learn

- Emotional storms can be a reaction to present circumstances and they can also be triggered by memories of the past. But however they came about, emotions contain messages about ourselves and our lives. When you feel up to it, investigate your feelings with an attitude of enquiry and compassion for your past and present suffering.

- *What challenge has brought on the feeling?*

- *What does it relate to?*

- *What does it show me?*

- *What is not yet resolved?*

- *Is the feeling stopping me from moving forward?*

- *What do I need to attend to?*

- *What can I learn about myself and the other people involved?*

For clarity the process is described as distinct steps but in reality the stages do not follow each other so neatly, they overlap and blend into each other. The emotions going through you will fluctuate - just like the wind and waves in a storm - but all you have to do is be aware of the emotion, acknowledging and staying with it without letting yourself drown, and later learning from it.

Processing your emotions in this way resolves them in the majority of cases. If they persist in a mild form or return from time to time, don't worry too much about it. No matter how much you know about them and how much inner work you have done, you may have to accept that you could be prone to certain emotions all your life. For example, if fear is an old buddy of yours it might flare up occasionally and sometimes even without obvious reason.

In such a case, don't get upset about the occurrence and dwell on the 'why' too much but watch it calmly as if it is something just passing through. It may have been brought about by a bit of indigestion or an automatic recollection of something disturbing, an image from a movie or nothing particular at all. In one such case, a person walked their dog on a lovely day on a tree-lined street and suddenly a feeling of anxiety popped up out of nowhere. Noticing it, the individual was perplexed but decided that it was not something to dwell on. Without further attention given to it, the fear was starved of energy and disappeared as inconspicuously as it had arrived.

Updates on the stories of Narelle and Dee (chapter 5), Wendy, Sue and John (chapter 2) and Simon (chapter 4)

It is common to respond to difficult experiences with one of the main survival emotions:

- fight: anger, irritation, frustration, antagonism, rage, aggression

- flight: anxiety, fear, nervousness, concern, worry, panic

- freeze: sadness, depression, disappointment, despondency, grief, gloom, despair

To manage their emotions, the individuals whose stories were told in part 1 applied the recommended strategies specific to their case as well as the general technique for dealing with emotional storms. Some of them may be prone to occasional relapse while others well and truly turned the corner:

Resolving anger: update on Narelle and Dee's story (chapter 5)
Following his serious sailing accident, Eric's mother Narelle and wife Dee turned against each other with aggressive fury. Both of them understood that his injuries posed a very real threat of permanent disability. Dee tried to cope with the 'danger' by limiting who could have access to him. For her, the mother - who

tended to be over-emotional - was an enemy she could control in a situation where everything else was beyond her control. For Narelle, Dee became the enemy excluding her from supporting her son.

If the two women had had a different history, they may have been able to pull together in female solidarity and comfort. Calmer times had allowed them to tolerate the other but in crisis that was not enough for mutual support and they only stopped fighting each other when the immediate threat to Eric's health diminished.

Dee relaxed her extreme gate-keeping and adopted a more inclusive attitude about Eric's contact with the wider family circle and friends. Narelle learned to moderate her emotions and tread lightly when interacting with her son's wife.

Both women realised that Eric needed peace in his life. Exhausted from the past struggles and hostilities, they accepted their differences and learnt to co-exist by keeping their distance from each other as much as possible but acting with civility when contact was inevitable.

Reducing overwhelming emotions, worry and panic: updates on Wendy, Sue and John's stories (chapter 2)

After the armed hold-up on the premises of the pharmaceutical company where they worked, the three employees suffered different forms of intense emotions that persisted even after the danger had long passed. Knowing how to ride out emotional storms helped them in two ways: as a separate exercise when overwhelming emotions began to rise or through practising it as part of the processes for self-soothing described in chapter 2.

John used it as part of the first-aid-for-panic technique while his fear was raging. In time, as his panic attacks became less severe in duration and intensity, John not only felt like his old self again but noticed with pride that he was much more in control of his emotions than he had been before. He even became a mentor for other colleagues when they struggled to cope with challenges and troubling emotions.

Sue never quite lost her predisposition to worry but learned to find her way through it before it took hold. Sometimes she even had to laugh at herself - always imagining the worst which then turned out to be a storm in a teacup!

Wendy hated that she had become so easily upset by even small things and resolved to do anything she could to get more control of her emotions. With determination and persistence she practised her favourite techniques until she could see results: after a few months her tendency to be overwhelmed by distressing emotions diminished and she was able to live in a much calmer way.

Overcoming depression: update on Simon's story (chapter 4)

Losing his job was like a death to Simon where his professional standing was destroyed and his future prospects looked bleak. He responded with depression, despondency and gloom. But with his partner's help, he realised that his depression did not have to become an ingrained mental health problem. It was simply a reaction to the situation imposed on him.

Overcoming the vicious cycle of negative thinking, emotions and physical neglect took time and effort but it changed his internal landscape. Even with substantial obstacles in his job search, he did not allow despair to take over. Instead he began considering different possibilities: perhaps establishing his own financial consultancy or combining his skills with those of Michelle to set up a new business partnership with her.

Don't forget humour

Humour is an essential component of resilience with benefits for physical, mental and emotional health. Germans have a word for humour in adversity: *'galgenhumor'*, that is the humour you have when facing the gallows. It sounds grim but highlights the fact that something comical can be found in the most unlikely situations.

It is essential for self-healing to take time out from duties, problems and from brooding about your difficulties. Leave upset and pain behind for a moment and notice the incongruous, comical, ludicrous or absurd in your situation. Give yourself permission for down time and play: funny stories, coffee with irreverent friends, the movies - not a disaster film! - a concert, drumming, anything spontaneous, creative and fun. Just enjoying yourself for a while will give your energies a much needed boost.

Guide posts

1. When in the grip of a strong emotion, use the strategy of riding out emotional storms.

2. For further reflection on your emotions, contemplate how they manifest in your body and mind as well, then choose which aspect to work on.

3. Remember to bring lightheartedness into your life.

Chapter 13

Be Who You Are

It is not always easy to be authentic and real. Most people have been 'taught' ideas about who they supposedly are or who they should be in order to be accepted, successful, safe or popular. They may have tried to be so many things for so many people that their identity has moulded itself around the messages they hear. They may suppress who they really are and hide behind a mask pretending to be someone they are not in their essence.

Being authentic includes backing yourself in the face of opposition, disapproval or potential exclusion. You may meet with criticism and disdain or no longer fit in. But if, for the sake of pleasing your 'tribe', you deny your true inclinations, talents, aspirations and values you are in danger of losing yourself in a false persona.

Know your authentic self

You may not be able to describe your authentic self with words. Instead there may be a feeling of being at home within yourself, of being whole, of having the right to be on this earth just as you are. Accepting your shadow as well as your light allows you to be all you are - quirky, weird, wonderful, exciting - without trying to be different, defending or protecting your individuality. When you are living in alignment with your inner self you:

- are comfortable in your own skin
- know and accept yourself
- make choices based on your own values and intentions
- map your own path in life
- feel no need to hide, pretend or defend
- dare to show real aspects of yourself even though they may not conform to other people's expectations
- are aware of your impact on others
- accept that not everyone will like who you are
- realise that as you evolve and change, maintaining precious authenticity may be a lifetime project

Authenticity can be an uncomfortable way of being. Liberating yourself from programs imposed by others will take time, effort, insight and self-awareness, however, practical steps in daily life will take you in the right direction.

Have courage and accept risk

- Be emotionally honest and express your feelings and opinions when appropriate.

- Be discerning about when and how you do it - letting it all 'hang out' is not always appropriate.

- Be aware of your true inclinations and step out of your comfort zone to express them.

- Set boundaries.

- Come out of hiding and put yourself out there.

- Dare to show real aspects of yourself.

- Accept being vulnerable and perhaps incur negative reactions.

- Know you are able to bounce back.

- Trust that like-minded people will connect with you.

- Stand up for yourself.

Use affirmations

When apprehensive or anxious about being more real, encourage yourself with affirmations to stay on track. Use the following examples or choose your own words to help you live an authentic life:

- *I am okay with criticism.*

- *I can handle rejection.*

- *Fear is just a feeling.*

- *I refuse to be what they want me to be.*

- *I find my own path.*

Align with your values

At the core of authenticity are the values you hold. They are deep convictions about the right way to live, interact with others, perform your job and generally conduct yourself. Many factors influence values: your childhood, the society you live in, people you look up to or socialise with, the media and advertising, social media or any other significant agency.

Most people are not really aware of their true values and perhaps you too find it difficult to describe them. Reflect on what feels right and what is important to you in areas such as family, partner/intimate relations, parenting, friendships/ social life/community, environment/natural world, career/ employment, recreation/fun/leisure, education/personal growth and development, health/physical well-being.

Some examples of values are: adventure, cooperation, creativity, equality, fairness, fitness, freedom, friendliness, generosity, honesty, humour, humility, independence, justice, kindness, intimacy, love, order, open-mindedness, patience, persistence, safety, self-awareness, self-control, sexuality, spirituality, supportiveness, trust.

Each person has their own set of values that inform their actions. For example, if you value cooperation you will treat other people with consideration, openness, the willingness to consider their point of view, courtesy and fairness. If self-control is of value to you, you will not let your emotions run rampant or smash dishes during an argument.

Living according to your values is not always easy. People close to you may have different values but in order to hold the peace you do not express yours. This is no problem if it is an occasional occurrence, however, if you deny them too often and in a fairly major way it creates internal dissonance between your own values and living a life contrary to them. An example would be a person who valued freedom and adventure but became locked into a life full of routine only to please another person. Sooner or later the dissonance of values will create psychological distress and will lead to the living of a very inauthentic life.

Trust your intuition

Intuition or the 'sixth sense' has had a rather chequered history. At various times it was considered a gift bestowed on only a few, a curse leading to persecution or a form of woo-woo imagination children were taught to suppress. Here it is treated as a valuable source of inner guidance.

Some individuals seem wired for strong intuitive abilities - as others are for athletic or musical talents - and can draw on great sensitivity to energetic clues: they are the mediums, clairvoyants, seers and prophets. Even people with less developed sensitivities have experienced a gut feeling, a hunch or sense of inner knowing.

Picking up subtle energetic clues from the environment, other people and even future events, intuition extends beyond the official five senses. Things are perceived and known, sometimes with inexplicable certainty, without conscious processing.

Intuitive knowing often comes out of the blue, as if suddenly a whole picture becomes visible in a flash of light or it is like a wordless inner whisper you can choose to ignore or listen to. There are many cases of people ignoring their whispers and paying quite a price for it later on: *I knew it wouldn't work out, but went ahead anyway, and now I've got to find a way out of this mess.*

If you do listen, intuition can be an invaluable tool to access your own truth and get more clarity on what is right for you. This can be very useful for making a decision. If you are unsure about a direction to take, your thoughts may be going round and round in circles, rapidly increasing self-doubt and uncertainty. To lift the confusion you can consult a different source of wisdom within you that goes deeper than normal mental considerations.

The process is not based on logic but can work in harmony with it. For example, after assessing a situation from different angles you can then also tune into your own inner compass. It will point you in the direction right for you based on your individual experience and perceptions, no matter what other people might want or what appears to be favourable at the time. Here is a strategy for accessing your own intuition:

1. Choose a time and space where you can be quiet and undisturbed.
2. Think of a question or something you want to contemplate.
3. Write the question down. Keep it simple: don't seek answers for life's greatest issues until you are comfortable with the technique and know you can trust your impressions.
4. Feel your feet in contact with the ground. Focus on the area of your heart. Breathe calmly and evenly. Let the body soften and release any tension. You should feel relaxed and comfortable, contained within yourself in a quiet receptive state of mind, gently tuning in to your own inner wisdom.
5. Hold your question lightly in your mind and wait. Don't force anything. Be open to whatever comes: it could be a feeling, words, ideas, knowings or thoughts that seem to come out of nowhere. If it remains hazy, give yourself a little nudge: *what is my real feeling about this?* Don't push, let answers arrive by themselves.
6. If it seems helpful, write down anything that will help you

remember what came up. Do not think about it, judge or dismiss it. Just record the information from inside you, nothing else.

7. Ask follow-up questions as they occur to you. Wait, be open to what comes and record.

8. When you feel finished, get back into your normal state and take a look at what you wrote down. Now you can analyse what came up in the process. Ask yourself questions such as: *does it feel true? Does it resonate with me? Does it seem the right answer/right way to go? Is it supported by what I already know about the situation? Does it feel right?* Keep probing to make sure the information and insights you received are valuable rather than fantasy. But whatever your next step, treat your new wisdom as a guideline rather than gospel to be followed blindly.

This process is not set in stone - you may decide on a different way of accessing your intuition. Whatever works for you is okay, however, if you are new to this approach, practising the above steps will help you become more proficient in tuning into yourself. Think of it as developing or strengthening your intuition muscles.

Don't be discouraged if you don't seem to be getting any worthwhile information or insights or if nothing happens at all. It is important to remember that intuition is a different sense to seeing, smelling or hearing. Sometimes you may not be in the right state for insight to flow or it may not be the right time. Intuition can not always be summoned at will, right there and then, when you search for its wisdom.

Nothing may happen during your session, but then in the

bus to work an insight pops into your head! Working with your own inner guidance requires patience and trust that one way or another the right answers will come to you if you remain open to that possibility. There is every chance that in time you will be able and confident to understand, evaluate and work with your intuition for thriving in life.

Love yourself

Self-love - really? Isn't it conceited, selfish, unpleasant, arrogant, narcissistic, vain and full of false pride? It is, if it is ego-based and full of self-importance. However, there is a different kind of self-love you really need.

This kind of self-love is spiritually based. With it you recognise your intrinsic value as a human being. You have respect for your life, time and energy. You nurture yourself with self-care. You do not allow others to take advantage of you or treat you badly. You accept yourself unconditionally with all your limitations. You treat yourself with a compassionate mindset.

There is no true self-love without authenticity, self-compassion and self-care. It means honouring yourself in all you do, not being afraid to be yourself, talking your talk and bravely walking your own path.

Count your treasures

Even if you think there is not a lot to love in your life, there is much to be grateful for. The road you have been on, and are travelling now has not only brought you hardship but many gifts as well.

Be proud of who you have become - wiser and stronger. Accept your courage and persistence in overcoming obstacles, setbacks and criticisms. Recognise what you have learned. Do you now have greater appreciation for life and pleasure in things that were once taken for granted? Increased closeness and depth in your relationships, with more empathy and compassion for other people's struggles? Have you found comfort and guidance from like-minded souls on a similar journey to you?

Notice the new perspectives, clarity and tolerance you have gained: how you look at people, events and yourself. Has your world view expanded so you no longer sweat the small stuff but give more time to the important things in life? If your experience did not result in questioning or losing your faith, has it strengthened or expanded your spirituality to include bigger questions about your existence, meaning and purpose?

Update on Lucy's story (chapter 1)

Lucy, who fell ill with a serious auto-immune disorder, realised that her sense of being victimised by fate was not helping her moods or her attempts at managing the illness. She recognised that although her vitality and strength were compromised, not all of her previous life had disappeared and much of her old self remained. She also discovered new things she could do that did not require much physical energy: painting, writing stories, sewing.

Finding treasures in her situation gave her the strength to keep going, reduced her stress and lifted her spirit. Focusing on things to love and be grateful for, Lucy paid attention to the smallest positive moments, joys or achievements - even writing them down in a gratitude journal. It transformed her from being a victim to being more than a survivor.

Choosing a life-affirming perspective on her illness, Lucy was able to improve her health. She managed herself with the same attitude of patience, kindness and tolerance she would have for a close friend. Exploring ways to boost her immune system and therapies suitable for her particular issues helped stabilise her condition.

Lucy still had a long way to go and perhaps would never again have quite the same seemingly unlimited resources of energy but she was no longer completely incapacitated and there was much hope that whatever limitations remained would not prevent her from living a satisfactory life.

Guide posts

1. Get to know yourself: your values, aspirations and talents.
2. Reflect on whether you live in alignment with your inner essence.
3. Trust your intuition as a valuable source of guidance.
4. Develop the kind of self-love that acknowledges your uniqueness and intrinsic value as a human being.
5. Look for the treasures in your circumstances.

Chapter 14

Claim Your Power

Each experience tells us something about ourselves, other people, the society we live in, the country, the world. You have been at the receiving end of problems and upheaval not of your choosing but the messages you receive from your experience - how you deal with it, how it changes you, who you become, what you learn from it - are entirely yours to choose. Consider this poignant native American story:

An old Cherokee said to his grandson who was full of anger at an injustice done to him: *'Let me tell you a story. I, too, at times have a great hate for those who have taken so much, with no sorrow for what they did. But hate wears you down and does not hurt your enemy. It is like taking poison and wishing your enemy would die. I have struggled with these and other negative feelings many times. It is as if there are two wolves inside me. One is evil, full of anger, envy, sorrow, regret, greed, arrogance, self-pity, guilt, resentment, inferiority, lies, false pride, superiority and ego. The other wolf is good, it is joy, peace, love, hope, serenity, humility, kindness, benevolence, empathy, truth, compassion and faith. It is hard to live with these two wolves, for both try to dominate my spirit.* The grandson thought about it for a while and then asked his grandfather, *Which wolf will win?* The old Cherokee replied, *The one you feed'.*

Difficult life changes create physical, mental, emotional and spiritual marks that give rise to the different wolves. Fostering a sense of personal power irrespective of the circumstances will help you choosing the good wolf.

The power of personal sovereignty

Countries are described as sovereign nations - but people? Personal sovereignty means being confident about one's own rights and place in the world. Acting from a position of knowledge, self-responsibility and strength, you exercise your power to make decisions about your own life and future.

You are the authority in your own life. Even though external events and circumstances are often beyond your control, nobody and nothing is able - unless you let them - to take away your free will over your inner life and response to life's challenges. In fact, free will, personal sovereignty and empowerment are so closely linked that one cannot exist without the others. Here is a list of key aspects to cultivate in order to strengthen and assert your personal sovereignty:

- self-awareness: recognising your emotions, thoughts and actions for what they are

- self-control: keeping emotions and impulses in check; being rational and realistic

- self-acceptance: knowing your abilities and limits, strengths and weaknesses and being okay about it

- self-confidence: a strong sense of self-worth and willingness to go beyond your comfort zone

- self-respect: having a backbone, setting boundaries and standing up for yourself

- self-determination: being goal-directed, charting your own path through life

- accountability: taking responsibility for your actions

- integrity: being trustworthy, conscientious, consistent, authentic

- social intelligence: considering the effects of your behaviour on others

- openness and flexibility: entertaining novel ideas and approaches

- self-care: protecting and directing your own energies wisely

Live with inner strength

Inner strength is created though effort and determination. At the core of it is the trust that one way or another you will be able to deal with whatever you encounter in life whether it is a serious crisis or simply the challenges of daily life.

If you do not let them crush you, hardship and adversity provide opportunities to strengthen your inner fortitude but you can also develop and strengthen it by deliberately enhancing key psychological attributes such as those listed below.

Beware a sense of entitlement to a trouble-free life. No one can claim exemption from hard knocks and unfulfilled expectations, hopes and dreams. An emotionally mature person deals with challenges with as much grace and competence as possible.

Strengthen your sense of self. Increase your self-knowledge and get to know how you tick. Be as honest and as objective as you can about your strengths and weaknesses, abilities and values.

Choose self-acceptance. It means being okay with your quirks and shortcomings, being authentic and real. Practise self-compassion when life has knocked you and self-forgiveness when you have not been your best.

See things as they are. Take stock of your circumstances bringing to mind the whole picture and taking the long view. View your current issues from an overall perspective and ask yourself how they fit into the big scheme of things.

Set boundaries. Know your values and limits. Bravely stand your ground when something is not acceptable to you.

Be aware of automatic negative thoughts. Instead adopt lateral thinking and looking outside the square. Be flexible and open to consider new options. Adjust to new developments. See problems as learning experiences that will help you become stronger and wiser.

Review your social life. Are you connected or dependent? Are you easily swayed and persuaded? Is the company you keep appreciating your individuality or do you have to change who you are to please others? Is there peer pressure to fit in? What is the group think? What are the 'shoulds' and demands to be a certain way? Whose values do you live by? Are you making your own choices and decisions or do you do what you think is expected of you?

Make sure to surround yourself with people who have values and goals that resonate with you and where there is mutual support and respect for the other. If necessary and possible stay away from toxic people who demean you or who try to clip your wings.

Become comfortable in your own company. Practise being alone and quiet, just with yourself. Only when you are able to be at peace with yourself will you develop the ability to be truly self-directed and self-reliant.

Manage your energies. Commit to self-care with healthy habits and practices. Inner strength is on shaky ground when your body is deprived of its true needs. You also need to be discerning about what you do and how you do it: when to persist, when to cut your losses and let go. But most of all, allow humour and light-heartedness. No matter how serious a situation, it is often possible to find something funny and to laugh at absurdities or even at yourself.

Resist drama and emotional turbulence. This requires a willingness to tolerate difficult feelings like sadness, disappointment, frustration, worry and fears. Fluctuations in mood are a normal part of life. While significant emotions should not be denied and need to be understood, with some degree of self-control you can keep your cool and stay strong.

Cherish spiritual connection. Whatever your religious beliefs, centre yourself in something bigger than yourself. Make time for Being, with moments where all Doing stops. Prayer, contemplation or tuning into universal energies will help you do that.

To develop and cultivate your own inner strength, choose from the above descriptions those areas where you are most lacking. Concentrate on one at a time. It may be challenging to step outside your comfort zone and expose yourself to failure and mistakes but that is part of becoming stronger. Do not be deterred by hiccups but transform yourself into a person who lives life from a position of inner strength.

Updates on the stories of Diane (chapter 6) and Sarah and Mike (chapter 9)

Rebuilding damaged self-esteem: update on Diane's story (chapter 6).

Diane, who was harassed not only at work but also in her social circle decided to take back her power and not let the bullies win. She began rebuilding herself in her own way, in private and in her own time, without telling anyone.

Her first small step was leaving the house to take the dog for a walk, which she had not done for a long time. To begin with she stayed close to her house, going only as far as she could cope without being totally overcome by anxiety. She also chose times when she knew that few people would be outside. Naturally, the dog was extremely happy and excited, which gave her a good feeling. Gradually she increased the length of the walk and moved further away from home, willing to tolerate the heightened level of anxiety and persist until it diminished.

In her dark time Diane had neglected her housekeeping duties but now she added one small job per day to get back into a routine. Her self-care and appearance had also deteriorated, drab clothes helping her recede into the background. Now she contemplated wearing bright colours and smarter outfits. What a brave move for someone who spent months in hiding, to step out in clothes not easily overlooked! Although she wondered whether that was too much too soon, it reminded her of who she once was and could be again. It felt scary but also exciting to take matters into her own hands even if only she knew of their significance.

A journal became Diane's new best friend. In it she reflected on the events and everybody's role in them. She realised the abuse was the action of a warped character and not because of anything she had done. She also understood that she had no control over people's opinion of her: all she could do was act with integrity and hold her head high. To strengthen her resolve, she made a list of affirmations:

- *I can be calm in social situations.*
- *I can handle it when people gossip.*
- *I am confident that I can deal with however people are.*
- *I decide who I respond to.*
- *I decide who I allow into my life.*
- *I am a good person.*
- *I am okay as I am.*
- *I believe in myself.*
- *I am strong.*

Diane's mood became brighter. At first hesitant and some-what timid in social situations, she nevertheless questioned her past compliance and need to please critical in-laws or community members. Trusting her own perceptions, her appraisal of people became more assured. Clarifying to herself what she found acceptable and how she wanted to relate, she learned to put up friendly but clear boundaries and took control of whom she let come close.

None of it happened overnight and many times it all felt too hard but Diane did not let herself be deterred by hiccups, setbacks and fears. She so wanted to get her power back!

Piece by piece Diane put herself together again and turned her life around. She reached out to her husband in a loving way and confided some of her past challenges. He had been aware of some issues but did not realise the severity of her experience. Much to her surprise he expressed unwavering support and stood firmly by her side until her integrity and morals were no longer questioned by their community.

The abuse by a perverse man nearly destroyed Diane. Having been so shattered and lost in terror made her question herself and her ability to cope. By overcoming crippling anxiety and shattered self-esteem she discovered strengths she never knew she had.

More than that, healing herself developed into a quest for authenticity. For the first time in her life Diane made judgments about what was right for her and how she wanted to be in her life. In the depth of despair and destruction, Diane found the seeds to her own individuality. From now on she could be her own person and thrive.

Asserting boundaries: update on Sarah and Mike's story (chapter 9).

The couple struggled with their daughter Erin's lack of consideration and respect when she moved back into their house with her young children. For fear of upsetting Erin and creating disharmony, Sarah and Mike initially tolerated her behaviour but resentment and stress made them realise they needed to draw on their inner strength, take their power back and stand their ground.

Addressing the difficulties in the home and applying the assertiveness strategies, Sarah and Mike communicated their concerns with calmness and determination. Erin was surprised about her parents' firm stand but had no choice but to consider their point of view. Being assured she and her children were welcome in their house gave her an extra impetus to make efforts for fitting in.

At times Erin and her parents 'relapsed': Erin not honouring their agreements and falling back into old habits of taking things for granted and Sarah and Mike feeling like victims in their own home. But with goodwill and cooperation they managed to resolve conflict before it got out of hand.

As an unintended consequence, the parents' new communication skills taught Erin valuable lessons in problem-solving and social interaction. Instead of reacting defensively or storming out of the room when things did not go her way she learned to listen and make her own points with firmness and clarity. This helped her greatly in finding and maintaining a part-time job while researching opportunities for future study.

Mike and Sarah were thrilled. The house was peaceful most of the time and they could enjoy their retirement as they had hoped.

Guide posts

1. To live with personal sovereignty, check which of its psychological attributes are already part of your functioning and strengthen those not yet well developed.
2. Trust your inner strength even in the most difficult of circumstances.
3. Take the initiative to claim your power.

Chapter 15

Be Comfortable With Change

There is a Buddhist practice of creating beautiful and intricate sand mandalas that get destroyed in a specific ceremony soon after completion. Why create something so full of meaning and beauty only to destroy it soon after? In their teaching, this seemingly paradoxical act symbolises the impermanence of life and confirms the view that the only certainty in life is change.

Practise psychological flexibility

Change is rarely a smooth ride where everything goes to plan. There are many uncertainties, unpredictabilities and hiccups on the way but whether change is exciting and welcome or frightening, confusing and stressful, whether it was imposed or chosen, you have to manage it. The more you are able to go with the flow of its progression, the less painful the process of change becomes.

Psychological flexibility includes lateral thinking, the ability or at least willingness to adapt to changed conditions and the resolve to tolerate discomfort. It is the opposite of being mentally rigid with fixed ideas, set expectations and unbending attitudes. To navigate change with psychological flexibility:

- Take a broad view of your circumstances with an attitude of inner detachment.

- Distinguish between what is important and what is not.

- Be willing to get out of your comfort zone.

- If one way does not work try another one.

- Remember there is more than one way to do things.

- Don't believe your fearful thoughts.

- Trust your resilience.

- Tolerate imperfection.

- Consider other people's comments or advice with discernment.

- Accept help when available.

Cultivate realistic optimism

Realistic optimism is not a blind 'she'll be right' attitude nor does it cling to magical thinking that someone or something will come and make it all better. This kind of optimism is the expectation of positive outcomes in difficult circumstances but without illusion about their likelihood.

Realistic optimism means accepting the consequences of adversity without succumbing to negativity about life and yourself, the event and your past, present and future. Even in seemingly insurmountable difficulties, you trust that options for positive developments exist and that you will find them although they may not be obvious at the moment. Below are some examples of how a realistic optimist might think:

About a difficult event

* *Although many doors have closed, there will be new openings and opportunities.*

* *I'll learn from it and move on.*

* *There is always something to make things better.*

* *It's okay to start again, you never know what's round the corner.*

About yourself

* *I know what I am capable of and when to call for help.*

* *I trust myself to create and take opportunities as they arise.*

* *I can redefine who I am.*

* *If I do not yet know how to do that, I will find out.*

However, guard against unrealistic optimism as overconfidence and impatience have no place in creating a new life. If you need to push past your comfort zone be gentle with yourself, realistically assessing your capabilities and options at any given time. Some things may have to wait for increased strength, external support and the opening-up of new opportunities.

Realistic optimism about yourself and your existence is at the heart of thriving in life. If one approach does not work, a realistic optimist will explore others. And if nothing can be done for a while obvious limitations will be accepted. With discernment, factual thinking, flexibility and constructive action, realistic optimism can guide you through challenges and adversity.

Your attitude affects your whole future. Choose the one that encourages action over stagnation, hope over despair, courage over avoidance and trust in yourself over giving up. Then tragedy will not break you but will lead to greater strengths and new blessings.

The basics of change

- **Small is good.** Breakthroughs and leaps forward are terrific when they occur but change mostly proceeds with one small step after the other.

- **Timing matters.** Sometimes, you might do everything right and throw yourself into the process with one hundred per cent commitment. Yet nothing happens, nothing seems to work out as if you are stuck in mud or there is no wind in your sails. That's where time comes in. Astrologers look to the stars to assess the right timing for taking action. Numerologists calculate numbers for the same reasons. You may not be inclined to that kind of thinking but the fact remains that sometimes things move forward with speed and ease and sometimes nothing shifts.

- **Change demands letting go of the past.** That does not mean forgetting or denying what happened or how it was then. It means accepting the current situation as the new reality and turning to the future with its different options.

- **Change is active.** Sitting at home waiting for someone to come or something to happen will not induce change.

- **Change thrives on determination and persistence.** This is especially true when the going gets tough or you need to pick yourself up after falling down.

- **Change needs boosters:** flexibility, lateral thinking, being bold and using all of your resources.

- **Change requires courage.** This means going beyond your comfort zone, facing the unknown, risking failure or the negative reactions of other people.

Prepare for difficult situations

From the early 1980s, Western mental-health practitioners have been developing new therapies based on the Eastern worldview that a person's well-being can be enhanced through techniques like yoga, tai chi, qi gong, meditation and others. Adapted for psychological treatment they may include tapping or holding certain acupuncture points on the body and taking specific postures, sometimes combined with talking about problematic issues or making positive affirmations.

Such techniques are based on the observation that shifting energies within the body influences health, emotions and state of mind. Collectively known as energy psychology or energy medicine, their effectiveness as self-help techniques for managing psychological stress is increasingly demonstrated.

A Hawaiian strategy, the Dynamind Technique (DMT) is one of the simplest practices. It can be harnessed to deal with psychological issues but many people have also found it useful as preparation for difficult situations. The technique is a combination of affirmation, intention and activating the energy system through conscious breathing, holding a gesture and tapping. Here is the formula in a nutshell:

1. *My problem is ...* (describing the issue)

2. *... and that can change.* (affirmation)

3. *Make it happen, make it so.* (intention)

4. Breathe, hand gesture, tapping, breathe. (activating the energy system)

5. Repeat and vary statement of the problem as needed.

This strategy can also be used as affirmation that you are capable of bringing about a desired result. Instead of stating the problem, you form a positive sentence: *I have the power to manage my fear. Make it happen, make it so.* Use it whenever you are doubting yourself and want to increase your confidence.

If you are with other people but feel the need to settle your emotions, you can use the technique quite inconspicuously. Hold the statements in your head instead of speaking and press the points with your fingers instead of tapping. Just pretend to be a bit fidgety and absorbed in your own world! If you need additional stability after a few rounds, focus on your feet and feel how solid they are on the ground (or your bottom on the seat), then say internally *relax* and keep breathing.

The technique sends signals to your energy system and teaches it to respond to your positive expectations. Don't be afraid of doing anything wrong: like all energy psychology strategies the method is very flexible and can be varied without compromising its effectiveness. Feel free to experiment to suit your needs and circumstances. Setting your intentions and tapping to reinforce them will give you a real sense of control.

Updates on the stories of Amanda (chapter 10) and Evan (chapter 7)

Initiating change: update on Amanda's story (chapter 10).

Amanda was determined to relocate to a less isolated residence despite her husband's resistance. She had finally found a house that suited her and that she believed would also meet Tom's expectations. But given her history of complying with his wishes rather than expressing her own, she dreaded having to confront him. Although she found the energy psychology technique described above rather strange, she decided to try it before confronting Tom:

1. Defining the problem. Amanda expected and feared a negative reaction from her husband when telling him about her intention of moving closer to town but now the time had come to discuss it with him.

2. Breathing. Amanda took a few breaths: in from the top of the head - imagining a light there and even touching the spot lightly with a finger.

Out through the feet - she found it helpful to wiggle her toes while breathing out.

3. Making a gesture. Amanda put the fingertips of both hands together and held it for a while.

4. Formulating your statements. Amanda described the problem she wanted to change: *I am really afraid of speaking to Tom and giving in if he refuses to deal with the issue.*

She then followed this with the affirmation: *And that can change. I want that problem to go away. Make it happen, make it so.*

5. Tapping. She reinforced the desired change by tapping seven times with three fingers of one hand in the centre of the chest, between the thumb and index finger (tap left and right hands) and on the big bone of the neck.

6. Breathing. Amanda again took a few conscious breaths in from the top of the head - imagining a light there and even touching the spot lightly with a finger. Out through the feet - wiggling her toes while breathing out.

7. Repeating. Amanda tuned into herself and noticed that there was not yet a real shift in her apprehension. She repeated the sequence several times. As she did this, she adjusted her statement or formulated new ones as they came to mind. For example, *Just thinking about Tom's reaction makes me shake and that can change. I want that feeling to go away. Make it happen, make it so.*

After practising this technique, Amanda felt calmer and more confident that she could handle Tom's reaction and stand her ground. He was most surprised by her newfound resolve and realising she would not budge, consented to look at the house and give it serious consideration.

Amanda used this technique - in private - before any subsequent discussion with Tom and in other circumstances as well. She found that by practising it frequently she was much more able to navigate change successfully. And happily, Tom eventually agreed to accommodate Amanda's wishes and move to the location and house of her choice.

Proceeding with realistic optimism: update on Evan's story (chapter 7).

Evan's relationships with his two ex-wives had deteriorated to such an extent that access to his sons became extremely difficult. Initially feeling powerless in the situation he realised that to change his circumstances he had to change himself.

It was not easy and took time, but eventually Evan's determined work paid off. He did not exactly make friends with his ex-wives but they came to find his support in raising the children useful and accepted his attempts at co-parenting. His new relationship with Nikki was developing and he began to be hopeful that his future could be very different from his past if he continued to be open to change.

Guide posts

1. Become psychologically flexible in your thinking and how you approach your situation.
2. Choose a perspective of realistic optimism.
3. Remember the basics of change.
4. Choose the strategies you most relate to and become a change master.

Chapter 16

Live With Intention

As a victim you believe yourself to be helpless, defeated and vulnerable. Self-pity may keep you rather passive, hoping to be rescued, feeding the 'evil wolf' energies. Your options seem very limited. You are preoccupied with the adversity and see it as defining your whole future in a very negative and restrictive way: *I'll never recover from this, it has destroyed my life.*

The problem with continuing to see yourself as a victim long after the event is that it maintains a painful and dysfunctional connection to an offender or adverse event. Blame, regret and anger will tie your focus to the past rather than to new opportunities in the future. Moving forward requires new thinking, flexibility and openness.

As a survivor you accept that despite life's knocks you have much of yourself left, got through it or are well on the way. You recognise your own potential to change and grow. Committed to moving forward, you use all of the skills, strengths and resources available to create a new life.

Justifiably proud about the progress you are making - often against the odds - you take brave steps towards a new future. But defining yourself as a survivor still takes the past event as a reference point for who you are now. Your identity is still tied up with what happened to you. Only when you move beyond the experience and commit to living your new life with optimism and empowerment can you become someone who thrives.

As a thriver you have not only gotten through or bounced back from adversity but are renewed, resilient and inspired by dreams for the future. You have made peace with the new circumstances. You find the positives in the new conditions and let them enhance your quality of life. Plans are developed, connections formed or renewed, possibilities explored and after a while the experience itself recedes into the background and you flourish in the new life you created.

Find meaning and purpose

Some individuals are so affected by their experience that they search for ways to find new meaning and purpose in life. As a result they undergo a transformation that turns them into a person almost unrecognisable to who they were before the incident. For example, they embark into territory never considered before: setting up charities, doing volunteer work, giving talks, creating art or writing a book.

Focused on issues greater than themselves, they use their adversity to contribute something valuable to the world and themselves. One such case is Rosie Batty, a quiet housewife and mother whose fourteen-year-old son was killed in front of her at a public sporting event by her violent former husband. Becoming a very prominent, outspoken and influential campaigner against domestic violence in the aftermath of this unfathomable horror, she gave new value to her son's and her own life.

Purpose provides a direction for life - you know what you want to express or achieve and look for ways of doing that. It is like the road to be travelled with goals as way stations along the way. When your chosen direction is significant and worthwhile to you, your life has meaning. It does not have to be spectacular or public, for example, people undergoing rehabilitation after an illness, accident or other serious impairment find new purpose in improving their health and setting up the conditions for the best kind of life possible in new circumstances.

In your own case, other people might try and tell you the direction to take and what your purpose should be. Don't be distracted or diverted: find what is right for you and makes you feel good about yourself. Choose your own road to travel. It may not be a smooth ride but it can bring new satisfaction and joy. To rewrite your life story and find your way towards new meaning and purpose, consider some of the following questions:

- *What is it that makes my life worth living?*

- *What do I really want from life?*

- *How could I use my experience in a positive way - for myself and/or for others?*

- *What would I like mentioned about me in a funeral service or etched into my gravestone?*

Your ideas do not have to be specific, they can be general: a feeling, longing for something better, a sense of overall direction and destination. It may be something bigger than yourself, a vision that energises and fills life with interest and challenge or you can be like an athlete working to improve their personal best and become the best version of yourself you can be.

Be present

Some people believe in always expecting the worst so they won't be hit so hard when things don't turn out well. Others don't allow themselves to plan for success so they won't feel bad when things turn out badly. Then there are individuals who avoid any kind of optimism because they are afraid of being disappointed.

It's a strange logic with a touch of superstition: expecting to feel bad later, they'd rather not feel good now. Worse still, such attitudes often become self-fulfilling prophecies. With so much attention given to negative expectations, how could anything positive find its way in?

Instead of being ruled by fearful anticipation, practise being present in the now. Similar to mindfulness, presence includes being grounded, aware of yourself, your surroundings and the people in them. It means being wholeheartedly engaged in what you are doing and what is going on right here, right now. You are in the moment physically, mentally and emotionally.

This might seem obvious but especially when doing routine or familiar tasks, like driving or washing up, it's easy for attention to drift away into dwelling on the past or future, imaginary scenarios or non-specific automatic mind chatter. When that happens, your awareness of what is going on and what you are doing at that moment is reduced. You spend time in your head rather than in the actual experience. The here and now is your real home and being there has many benefits.

Increased awareness provides useful feedback about what is going on and allows you to make better decisions and take effective action. You can be more confident as you are actually 'there' to deal with issues and apply yourself fully to what the situation requires. Being present and giving other people your full attention is also important for establishing and maintaining good relationships. Above all, it gives you the ability to live a conscious self-directed life.

Update on Brooke's story (chapter 3)

After the sudden death of their beloved Don and contemplating potentially malevolent involvement from his wife, Don's sister Brooke and their parents found it difficult to move beyond their own grief. The plight of his little daughter with whom he had been so close and who now remained overseas with her mother was all but overlooked. But once the family were made aware to look at the girl as his legacy, rather than as merely the offspring of a woman viewed with suspicion, the floodgates opened.

As if emerging from a long nightmare, Brooke and her parents dared open their minds to the new possibility of honouring their lost son by supporting his daughter in every way. Their devastating loss contained the potential for new meaning and purpose. Accepting that they might never know the full truth about the circumstances surrounding Don's death, they ceased speculating about it and turned their attention to the future.

They were a close-knit family and the little girl had always fitted in very well. What if she were to come and live with them? For the sake of the girl, contact with her mother would be maintained but by fully integrating her into his family of origin many of Don's dreams for his little girl could come true.

After some time this became a reality. Despite her detachment, Don's wife had always supported visits by the child to her Australian grandparents and did not object to the girl relocating. For Don's daughter, being welcomed into her beloved father's family in Australia helped her come to terms with her own loss and fears for the future.

Guide posts

1. Allow the experience to transform you.
2. Open the door to new meaning and purpose.
3. Live your life with presence and intention.

Final Words

▶ ▶ ▶

Getting from being a victim to becoming a survivor and ultimately thriver is different for each person. The chapters in this book have presented a smorgasbord of psychological qualities that could be helpful on the way, with some standing out as essential tools for effectively managing life and its challenges.

Make sure your psychological toolkit is up to date

Appreciate your uniqueness. From Dr. Seuss:

> *Today you are you!*
> *That is truer than true!*
> *There is no one alive who is you-er than you!*

Appreciate and value what makes you You - even if you are not like others, have changed after your experience or completely redesigned your life. If it is not a good fit for you, there is no place for trying to be like others or conforming to how they do things.

The more authentic you are, the more you are able to walk your own path. Accept and love yourself without false modesty.

Accept reality. You see things as they are rather than as you wish them to be or have been told they are. You have no illusions about the situation you are in. You look at the facts of the event: Was there malicious intent? Was it an accident that could have happened anywhere? Were you in the wrong place at the wrong time with the wrong people? Is it likely to happen agin?

Your decisions and priorities are based on what seems possible at the time. If other people are involved, you assess their capabilities and attempt to place them accordingly. You are aware of your own strengths and limitations.

Take responsibility. What happened may have been beyond your control but your reactions can be chosen by you. Will you let it define your life forever or is it a temporary roadblock requiring a detour? Will it push you into loss of hope and helplessness or is it a call to action for rebuilding and renewal? You claim your power, even if it is hard to do.

Look at your thoughts. Which ones are you listening to: the automatic ones that tend to obsess and ruminate about what happened or thoughts you choose to focus on deliberately? You are discerning and only trust the thoughts that are true or at least realistic. You refuse to give energy to those that drag you down and instead choose those that can direct you forward.

Tame your emotions. It's natural to respond with strong emotions to adverse and very challenging events. You make sure yours are not clouding your thinking or turning your life toxic, reducing your options and keeping you stuck in the past. You use the 'gang of three' - emotions, mind and body - to your advantage and become adept at riding out emotional storms.

Gather your courage. This involves getting out of your comfort zone into unknown territory. You do not let fear stop you or cause you to hide: you know what you want and proceed in spite of it.

Tolerate uncertainty. Life does not come with a roadmap or manual - although sometimes it would be helpful to have one! Left to find your own way, you accept that confusion and not knowing are all inevitable parts of the journey.

Accept mistakes, failures and dead ends. Life is full of moments that trip us up. But instead of being bowled over you shrug them off or use the hiccups for learning about yourself. You accept that being human means you are not - and don't have to be - perfect. You know you are not always your best. And you are okay with that.

Be flexible. What happens in life cannot be controlled but you can master your relationship with it by taking advantage of openings and opportunities, undeterred by difficulties and mapping your own path forward. If external events or people have pushed you into turbulent currents that are difficult to navigate, you seek more information, modify your approach, try something else and review your attitude.

Become solution focused. Once you accept the new reality, withdraw attention from focusing on problems. Instead you direct it at ways to move forward - even if they are very small steps - and become proactive in creating a new life.

Bounce back. If things go wrong or you are facing major

challenges, you don't give up. You know that whatever happens there is always something positive to work with. You are able to pick yourself up and keep going, even if it is in a different direction than before.

Develop determination and persistence. Half-hearted attempts rarely get you where you want to go. You understand that road blocks and challenges are normal, you are not deterred by them. You know when it is wise to cut your losses, but do not give up prematurely. The saying *'When the going gets tough, the tough get (keep) going'* applies to you.

Have patience. If things seem to take forever, you hang in there and don't use it as an excuse to withdraw. Sometimes events unfold in their own time but there is always something else you can do while a project is on hold. Transitioning from victim to survivor to thriver is not an even path; there will be ups and downs. Progress may be slow and difficult and require much determination and persistence but you hang in there.

Practise self-care. You know that to function well you need to look after yourself mentally, emotionally and physically. You make sure to get enough sleep, rest and eat quality food. And have fun!

- Seek out opportunities to nourish yourself and replenish your energies.

- Set up routines and structure your life to create stability.

- Build good health habits: sleep, food, activities.

- Engage in physical activities to release hormones for well-being and loosen 'stuckness' in body, mind and emotions.

- Simplify your life to help you focus on essentials.

- Connect with positive people.

- Spend time appreciating the beauty of nature.

- To really unscramble your energies and keep them humming, consider Donna Eden's 'Daily Energy Routine' (choose the original version on Youtube).

Keep the big picture in mind. If needed, create some slogans:

- It's a big (difficult) change, but there are options.

- Other people have gone on and made a good life for themselves.

- Life may be different but can still be satisfying and interesting.

- I have overcome other hurdles, I can do it again.

- I have power in this situation.

Best wishes for your journey of recovery, rebuilding and ultimately thriving. May this book be a call to action for self-transformation and empowerment so the seeds contained in adversity will turn into a life of new blessings and joy.

Live with intention.
Walk to the edge.
Listen hard.
Practice wellness.
Play with abandon.
Laugh.
Choose with no regret.
Appreciate your friends.

Continue to learn.

Do what you love.

Live as if this is all there is.

Poem by Mary Anne Radmacher

Further Reading

Borysenko, Joan. (2009). *It's not the end of the world. Developing resilience in times of change.* New York: Hay House.

Brantley, Jeffrey. (2007). *Calming your anxious mind. How mindfulness and compassion can free you from anxiety, fear and panic.* Oakland, CA: New Harbinger Publications.

Brown, Brene. (2015). *Rising strong. If we are brave enough, often enough, we will fall.* London: Vermillion.

Denise, Jan. (2008). *Innately good. Dispelling the myth that you're not.* Deerfield Beach, Fl: Health Communications Inc.

Eden, Donna. (2008). Energy Medicine. Balancing your body's energies for optimal health, joy and vitality. London: Penguin.

Grant, Anthony M., Greene, Jane. (2001). *Coach yourself. Make real change in your life.* Edinburgh: Pearson Education Ltd.

Joseph, Stephen. (2011). *What doesn't kill us. The new psychology of post traumatic growth.* New York: Basic Books.

McKay, Matthew., Rogers, Peter D., McKay, Judith. (2003). *When anger hurts. Quieten the storm within.* Oakland, CA: New Harbinger Publications.

Neff, Kristin. (2011). *Self compassion. Stop beating yourself up and leave insecurity behind.* London: Hodder & Stoughton Ltd.

O'Hanlon, Bill. (2011). *Quick steps to resolving trauma.* New York: W.W.Norton & Company.

Richo, David.(2005). *The Five things We Cannot Change … and the Happiness We Find by Embracing Them.* London: Shambala.

Schiraldi, Glenn R. (2007). *10 simple solutions for building self-esteem. How to end self-doubt, gain confidence & create a positive self-image.* Oakland, CA: New Harbinger Publications.

Schlossberg, Nancy K. (2008). *Overwhelmed. Coping with life's ups and downs.* Lanham, Maryland: M. Evans.

Tipping, Colin C. (2000). *Radical forgiveness. Making room for the miracle.* Dublin: Gateway.

Wehrenberg, Margaret.(2010). *The 10 best-ever depression management techniques. Understanding how your brain makes you depressed & what you can do to change it.* New York: W.W. Norton & Company.

Wehrenberg, Margaret.(2008). *The 10 best-ever anxiety management techniques. Understanding how your brain makes you anxious & what you can do to change it.* New York: W.W. Norton & Company.

Think Like a Monk
Jay Shetty (2020).

Heart Healing (2018).
Susyn Reeve

About the Author

Christiana Star (BA Hons Psychology, BA Hons Education) is a registered psychologist, writer and former teacher.

At the start of her professional life in Hamburg, Germany, Christiana taught in schools and teachers' colleges, participated in the curriculum development team of the Department of Education and administered statewide IQ tests.

Beginning a new life in Sydney, Australia, Christiana trained as a psychologist and established a private practice working also as a corporate consultant, EAP (employee assistance) provider, critical incident counsellor and facilitator of public workshops and seminars.

Christiana's writing draws on the skills of both professions. Her extensive experience and expertise as a psychologist led to a deep understanding of psychological pain, its impact and the complex issues of managing difficult life challenges. Christiana's approach is solution-focused, multidisciplinary and based on a spiritual outlook on life. Using her teaching skills to create easy to understand materials for self-help, empowerment and personal growth, her practical and effective resources are for everyone who wants to achieve personal transformation and success on their own terms.

To access more of Christiana's work, be informed about new projects and generally stay in touch, visit christianastar.com.